# NEAR-DEATH EXPERIENCE: SCIENTIFIC INTERPRETATION

*(Inspired by True Story of a Friend)*

Prof. (Dr.) Jai Paul Dudeja

INDIA • SINGAPORE • MALAYSIA

# CONTENTS

# PREFACE

Dear Readers,

I am extremely happy to see this book titled, **"Near-Death Experience: Scientific Interpretation (Inspired by True Story of a Friend)"**, in your hands. It is my firm belief that you have chosen to read this book with a specific aim in mind, and I assure you that you will not be disappointed with it.

A near-death experience (NDE) is the conscious, semi-conscious or recollected experience of someone who has been declared 'clinically dead' by the doctors, followed by resuscitation (the act of bringing someone back to life).

Common traits that have been reported by NDErs (persons having near-dear experiences) are: A sense/awareness of being dead; A sense of peace, well-being, painlessness and other positive emotions; a sense of removal from the world; an intense feeling of unconditional love and acceptance; experiencing euphoric environments, an out-of-body experience (OBE); that means, a perception of one's body from an outside position, sometimes observing medical professionals performing resuscitation efforts; a "tunnel experience" or entering a zone of darkness; a sense of moving up, or through, a passageway or staircase; A rapid movement toward a bright light; being reunited with deceased loved ones; receiving a 'life review', commonly referred to as "seeing one's life's flash-back before one's eyes"; approaching a border or a decision by oneself or others to return to one's body, often accompanied by a reluctance to return; and suddenly finding oneself back inside one's body.

Although majority of the NDErs report pleasant experiences, a few of them may have distressing or unpleasant experiences also.

This book consists of **13 chapters, categorized into three sections**: (i) Introduction, (ii) True Stories, and (iii) Scientific Interpretation.

**Section-I** (chapters 1-4) is about the Near-Death-Experience (NDE): Introduction and Overview.

**Section-II** (chapters 5-8) is about the NDE: Some True Stories.

**Section-III** (chapters 9-13) is about the NDE: Scientific Interpretation.

The author sincerely believes that a book of this nature will be appreciated by all the readers across the globe who wish to get a deep insight into various aspects of the Near-Death Experiences (NDEs), their scientific interpretation and utilization for their personal enlightenment.

The author would open heartedly love to receive any encouraging/ critical comments as well as feedback from the dear readers at his Email ID: drjpdudeja@gmail.com

Sincerely

**2023**                                         **Prof. (Dr. ) Jai Paul Dudeja**

# ACKNOWLEDGEMENTS

The seeds of my interest in spirituality and mysticism were lovingly sown by my revered parents: **Late (Dr. ) Shanti Sawrup Dudeja and (Late) Mrs. Jai Devi Dudeja**. I am sure that they are watching me every moment from wherever they are in the other world and continuously sending their blessings to me.

This book is humbly dedicated to Guruji of Bade Mandir, who constantly inspires and protects tens of millions of his devotees even today, after he left his body in 2007.

I have greatly benefitted in going through the books and articles referred in the 'Bibliography' in this Book. I gratefully acknowledge these authors for enhancing my understanding on the subject matter of this book.

My greatest admiration is reserved for **Mrs. Rita Dudeja**, my wife and my best friend. She is a continual source of inspiration for me and is a co-traveller on this path of trust and truth.

2023                                              **Prof. (Dr. ) Jai Paul Dudeja**

# INSPIRATION

The inspiration to write this book came from the true story of a very dear friend of mine who had felt a 'Near-Death-Experience (NDE) recently. He is an ardent devotee of a Guru. When I requested my friend to share his details with the authors of this book, he politely declined as he did not want to commercialize and publicize his situation (in the form of this book) with my readers; keeping the sanctity and discipline taught by his Guru. Consequently, in order to honour his wishes and sentiments, I am producing herewith sketchy details of his story (by hiding his name and other details) and the name of his hospital etc., in the following:

My friend was admitted to the Emergency Ward of a famous hospital in New Delhi in 2023 for angiography followed by stenting at a very critical life-threatening area. For more than two hours after admission, this procedure didn't succeed. So, it had to be discontinued. The doctors suggested that the only possible way out, though extremely risky, was to use the impella-support device during the time stent is inserted at the blocked place. After procuring this device, the procedure was started again, which once again went totally wrong, and my friend was declared 'clinically dead', with zero BP and all the monitoring parameters going dead. But, by the grace of his Guru (as he claims), he again pulled through and came back to life. Another few hours later, the stent was put in its desired place. After getting discharged from the hospital, his surgeons asked him 'how was the death experience, what he saw, and how he felt', etc.!

# PROFILE OF THE AUTHOR

Born in June 1948, Prof. (Dr. ) Jai Paul Dudeja holds a brilliant academic record. He did his Master's degree from Birla Institute of Technology and Science (BITS), Pilani (India), and Ph.D. degree from the Indian Institute of Technology (IIT), Delhi. He has been in regular employment as a Scientist, Professor, Dean, Director, Principal and a Senior Administrator in various educational institutions, universities, laboratories, public and private organizations. He superannuated as a Senior Scientist and Additional Director in May 2008 from the Defence Research and Development Organisation (DRDO), Government of India. After DRDO, he served for over 11 years, till his last posting as a Director at Amity University Gurgaon, from where he retired in Nov 2019.

Till date, Dr. Dudeja has published/presented about 90 research papers in various national and international journals/conferences. Out of these, over 20 research papers are on spirituality and consciousness etc. Besides this, he has authored the following **twenty-two books** on spirituality and consciousness:

1. Gayatri Mantra: A GPS to Enlightenment,

2. Maha Mrityunjaya Mantra: An Invincible Armour for Conquering Death

3. Ajapa-Japa Sohum-Humsa Mantra: An Eternal Mantra for Inner Consciousness

4. The Third Eye: A Spiritual Laser for Stimulating Inner Awakening

5. Quantum Physics of Consciousness and Non-Duality in Eastern Philosophy

6. Quantum Science of Love, Healing, Happiness, and Bliss in Ancient Wisdom

7. Chakras Healing and Kundalini Awakening by Yogic Techniques,

8. Meditation Practices across the Globe and their Beneficial Effects.

9. Comparative Analysis of Hindu, Buddhist, and Jain Philosophies

10. Mantras for Happiness

11. Om Namah Shivaya: A Powerful Mantra for Mastering Five Elements

12. Trataka: A Concentrated Gazing Technique for Mystical Powers

13. Walking Meditation: Techniques and Benefits

14. Quantum Science of Ganesha Consciousness

15. Tantra Science

16. Quantum Brain, Mind, and Thinking

17. Profound Meditation Techniques in Tibetan Buddhism

18. REIKI: A Holistic Energy Healing Technique

19. SHAKTIPĀT: Instant Transmission of Spiritual Energy from a Siddha Guru to the Disciple.

20. Vāstu Shāstra: Ancient Indian Science of Architecture

21. Vedantic Thoughts on Māyā, Mithyā, and the Brahman

22. Siddhis (Supernatural Powers): A Guide for Understanding and Attaining These

Dr. Dudeja has delivered many invited lectures in international conferences on 'Spirituality and Consciousness' in India and abroad.

He has been initiated to more than half-a-dozen meditation techniques.

Dr. Dudeja has been recognized as the "World's Who's Who in Science & Engineering".

# SECTION-I

# NEAR-DEATH-EXPERIENCE: INTRODUCTION AND OVERVIEW

# NEAR-DEATH EXPERIENCE: INTRODUCTION AND OVERVIEW

## 1.1 What is Near-Death Experience (NDE)?

A near-death experience (NDE) is the conscious, semi-conscious or recollected experience of someone who has been declared 'clinically dead' by the doctors, followed by resuscitation (the act of bringing someone back to life). People who recall near-death experiences have described perceiving a variety of events, such as seeing themselves from above or passing through a tunnel of darkness, etc.

Some of the general features of the near-death experience (NDE) include: impressions of being outside one's physical body (out-of-body experience or OBE), visions of deceased relatives and religious figures. Many such experiences have been reported, although the person's interpretation of these events often corresponds with the cultural, philosophical, or religious beliefs of the person experiencing it.

### 1.1.1 Common Traits of NDE

Common traits that have been reported by NDErs (persons having near-dear experiences) are:

- A sense/awareness of being dead.

- A sense of peace, well-being, painlessness and other positive emotions.

- A sense of removal from the world.

- An intense feeling of unconditional love and acceptance.

- Experiencing euphoric environments.

- An out-of-body experience (OBE). That means, a perception of one's body from an outside

  position, sometimes observing medical professionals performing resuscitation efforts.

- A "tunnel experience" or entering a zone of darkness.

- A sense of moving up, or through, a passageway or staircase.

- A rapid movement toward a bright light.

- Being reunited with deceased loved ones.

- Receiving a 'life review', commonly referred to as "seeing one's life's flash-back before one's eyes",

- Approaching a border or a decision by oneself or others to return to one's body, often accompanied by a reluctance to return.

- Suddenly finding oneself back inside one's body.


Note that an **OBE may or may not be part of an NDE**; it can happen in other instances also, such as fainting, deep sleep, alcohol or drug use.


### 1.1.2   Five Stages of NDE

NDEs can be subdivided in the following five-stage continuum.

These subdivisions are:

  (i)   Peace,

  (ii)   Body separation,

  (iii)   Entering dark tunnel,

  (iv)   Seeing the bright light, and

  (v)   Entering another realm of existence, through the light.

### 1.1.3    Perceptions of Life after NDE

NDEs are associated with changes in personality and outlook on life after these experiences. Among these changes, are:

(i)    greater appreciation for life,

(ii)    higher self-esteem,

(iii)    greater compassion for others,

(iv)    less concern for acquiring material wealth,

(v)    a heightened sense of purpose and self-understanding,

(vi)    desire to learn,

(vii)    elevated stage of spirituality,

(viii)    greater planetary concern,

(ix)    a feeling of being more intuitive,

(x)    no longer worrying about death, and

(xi)    claiming to have witnessed an afterlife.

Following are detailed experiences of life after death of an NDEr:

## 1.2    Some Experiences of those who have gone through NDEs

### 1.2.1    Ineffability (Indescribability) of NDE

Those who have gone through NDEs, characterize their experiences as ineffable or inexpressible. It is as if all the words that we have are three-dimensional, while the next world is definitely not three-dimensional.

### 1.2.2    Hearing the voices of persons around

Many of the persons, who have gone through NDEs, hear the voices of their doctors, nurses or bystanders exclaim loudly about their being dead, to the extent that they (the NDErs) can faithfully reproduce the exact words spoken by them.

### 1.2.3 Feelings of Peace and Quietness

Many people describe extremely pleasant feelings and sensations during the early stages of their experiences. Their pain vanishes and is replaced by feelings of peace, quietness, relief, comfort, ease, solitude and relaxation.

### 1.2.4 The Noise or Music

There are various unusual auditory sensations. Sometimes these are unpleasant and are described as buzzing, loud ringing, a loud click, a roaring, a banging and as a whistling sound like the wind. In other cases, they hear pleasant music like the tingling of Japanese wind bells or majestic, beautiful sort of music.

### 1.2.5 The Dark Tunnel

Often concurrently with the noise or music, people have the sensation of being pulled very rapidly through a dark space of some kind. This has been variously described as a cave, a well, a trough, an enclosure, a tunnel, a funnel, a vacuum, a void, a sewer, a valley, or a cylinder. It has been compared to a ride on a roller coaster train at an amusement park, a journey through a tunnel of concentric circles, or going down a very dark path in a very deep valley.

### 1.2.6 Out-of-Body (OBE)

When they (NDErs) move out of their physical bodies, they are in for an overwhelming surprise. They find themselves looking at their own physical bodies from the outside as though they are the spectators, a third person in the room or watching figures in a play or a film. They are quite confused and do not link it with death for some time. Some would like to get back into their physical bodies, as they do not know how to proceed further. Some have concern for their bodies and would not like these to be used as cadavers (dead bodies). Some take time to recognize their own bodies, as they are used to looking at themselves from the front in a mirror. Others have no feelings at all towards their bodies.

At some stage, the persons realize that they have died. Some welcome this realization. Others react with bafflement and even a certain refusal.

One or two persons found that they had been released from their bodies and felt that they were now pure consciousness, without occupying any space. But the majority found themselves into a new body, which might be referred to as the 'spiritual body'.

Most people find the human language inadequate to describe their 'spiritual body'. But there is a similarity in their accounts about the basic features of this body.

The person (NDEr) is both inaudible as well as invisible to others. His body seems to lack solidity. Physical objects appear to move through it with ease, while he is unable to get a grip on any object or person he tries to touch. The body is weightless. He seems to be floating right up to the ceiling of the room or into the air. Quite a few were aware of the lack of the physical sensations of body weight, movement and position.

All these features can also be looked upon as the absence of limitations. He (the person who has undergone NDE) can see and hear other persons, but the they cannot see or hear him. He can cross any physical entity like a door or a wall with ease. Movement from one place to another can be extremely rapid, almost instantaneous.

The spiritual body has a shape or form, sometimes a globular or amorphous cloud and sometimes essentially the same shape as the physical body. It also seems to have parts (projections or surfaces analogous to arms, legs, a head etc.). It is often said to have ends, a definite top and bottom.

The spiritual body has been variously described as a mist, a cloud, smoke-like, a vapour, transparent, a cloud of colours, wispy, an energy pattern etc.

Almost all accounts remark on the timelessness of the out-of-body state. It is almost as if time is standing still. Also, people seem to think more lucidly and rapidly than in physical existence.

On or two subjects had no sensation of temperature, while most people felt comfortably warm. No one reported any odors or tastes while out of their bodies.

The senses of sight and hearing seem to be heightened and more perfect. Vision seems incredibly more powerful. They can see very far, as if they could look anywhere and everywhere. If they want to see something at a distance, they sort of zoom up to it. Part of the body seems to go there like a tracer.

Hearing is called by that name only by analogy. They do not really hear physical voices or sounds. They seem to pick up the thoughts of persons around them and there is a direct transfer of thoughts. They seem to know what the others are thinking, but only in their minds.

Even severe damage to the physical body does not seem to affect the spiritual body adversely.

As they are unable to speak or touch other people, they have a tremendous sense of loneliness and isolation. They may sometimes feel depressed at this failure to communicate with others.

### 1.2.7   Meeting Others

This feeling of isolation does not last long, as very soon the subject sees or meets or hears other spirits or spiritual beings, who comfort him or answer his queries. Sometimes they reveal themselves as guardian spirits or spiritual helpers. They are apparently there to ease him through his transition into death or tell him that his time to die had not yet come. The subject recognizes many relatives and friends who have already died. It seems to him to be a joyous occasion like a homecoming.

### 1.2.8   The Being of Light

The element which has the most profound impact on individuals is their encounter with a very bright light. At first the light is dim, but it rapidly gets brighter till it reaches an unearthly brilliance. Although the light is white or clear, it does not hurt their (NDErs') eyes or dazzle them or keep them from seeing other things around them.

They refer to it as a being of light, a personal being as it has a definite personality. It exudes love and warmth which completely surround the subject and puts him at ease. He feels accepted and is irresistibly drawn to the being.

The identity of the light is determined by the religious background of the person involved. Christians identify the light as Christ. A Jewish couple identified it as an angel. No one claimed that the being had wings, played the harp or even had a human appearance.

The being starts to communicate with the person through a direct, unimpeded transfer of thoughts, in a clear way with no scope for misunderstanding or of lying to the light. The being asks a question which has been variously translated as "Are you prepared to die?" "Are you ready to die?", "What have you done with your life to show me?" and "What have you done with your life that is sufficient?"

The questions are not about preparation and accomplishment. It is a single question which the being asks whether the individual is satisfied with the way he has lived till then and whether he is prepared to die. The question is not asked to accuse, threaten or condemn the individual concerned. There is a feeling of total love and acceptance, whatever his answer might be. It is a Socratic question, asked not to elicit information but to help him to proceed along the path by himself.

### 1.2.9 The Life Review

The questions posed by the being of light are the prelude to a moment of startling intensity, during which the being presents to the person a panoramic review of his (NDEr's) life. It is obvious that the being can see the individual's whole life displayed and he himself does not need information. His only intention is to provoke reflection.

This review is extraordinarily rapid. The memories follow one another swiftly either in chronological order or without any temporal order. The remembrance is instantaneous and the individual is able to take it all in one mental glance. The experience is over in an instant of earthly time. The review is a display of visual imagery and is incredibly vivid and real. Sometimes the images are reported to be in vibrant colour, three-dimensional and even moving. Although they are flickering rapidly, each image is perceived and recognized. Even the emotions and feelings associated with the images may be reexperienced as one is viewing them.

As they witness the display jointly, the being seems to stress the importance of two things: learning to love other people and acquiring knowledge. The being points out that one should try one's best to do things for other people. Even when certain negative features are seen, he does not make any accusation. His attitude is that one learns from such experiences too. The being stresses the need to continue learning, which keeps on happening even after death.

Sometimes the review takes place without the being, but the review done in his presence is a more overwhelming experience.

## 1.2.10   The Border or Limit

In a few instances, persons (NDERs) seem to be approaching what might be called a border or limit of some kind. This has taken the form in various accounts of a body of water, a grey mist, a door, a fence across a field or simply a line. These could possibly represent varying individual ways of interpreting, wording or remembering the root experience.

## 1.2.11   Coming Back to the Physical Body

The most common feelings in the first few moments following death are a desperate desire to get back into the body and an intense regret over one's demise. But once the dying person reaches a certain depth in the experience, he normally does not want to get back. This is especially the case for those who have encountered the being of light.

The reluctance is because of the wonderful feelings of calm, joy and ease in the presence of the being. Some of them return voluntarily, because they have left some task such as education unfinished, or would like to look after their children or an ailing spouse. They feel that they have themselves voluntarily taken the decision to return and God has permitted them because of the unselfish motive they had. One young mother was mystified whether God had sent her back to look after her two small children or because he did not find her fit to be let into heaven.

In a few cases, they had been pulled back because of the prayers of their loved ones.

About the manner of return, there are different experiences. Some fall asleep and wake up in their bodies. Others are brought back rapidly with a jerk. In one case, the person felt that his spiritual body seemed to have a large and a small end. When it left the physical body, it seemed that the large end left first. Coming back in, the small end seemed to come in first.

Typically, the moods and feelings associated with the experience are so wonderful and indescribable that these linger on for quite some time.

### 1.2.12   Telling Others

Most of the subjects (NDErs) were persons having stable personalities and they were fully capable of distinguishing between a dream, a fantasy, a hallucination and a real experience. They were very clear in their mind that they had had this experience while in a normal frame of mind and that they had not made it up.

They realize that our contemporary society is just not the environment where such stories would be received with sympathy and understanding. They feel that if they narrated their experiences, most people would wonder whether they had lost their minds. If they tried, people looked at them as if they were crazy.

It was, therefore, not surprising that most people had the notion that they were unique and no one else had undergone what they had. But when they were informed that others had reported exactly the same events and perceptions, they expressed profound feelings of relief. They realized that they were not crazy or mentally deranged.

Some were also reticent because the experience was so indescribable, so far beyond human language, that it was fruitless even to try.

### 1.2.13  Effect on Lives

The effect of the experiences seemed to be that their lives had been broadened and deepened by the experience. They became more reflective and more concerned with ultimate philosophical issues. They realized that there was more to life than Friday night movies and football matches. They started acting after due reflection and not in selfish terms as they used to do before NDE. Life became much more precious for them. They started concentrating on the present rather than brooding on the past. They now gave less importance to the body and more to the mind.

Some of them developed certain intuitive faculties bordering on the psychic. They had a calming effect on others. They were more in tune with people. They could read faces and guess that some people needed help. They could pick up people's thoughts.

Most of them learnt some lessons, especially about the importance of cultivating unselfish love and seeking knowledge. They decided not to stop learning, as learning was a process that went on till eternity.

Their vision left them with new goals, new moral principles and a renewed determination to try to live in accordance with them, but with no feelings of instantaneous salvation or of moral infallibility.

### 1.2.14  Changed Views of Death

The NDE experience has a profound impact on the way people perceive physical death. They are no longer afraid of it. They do not actively seek death or wish to commit suicide, but they are firmly convinced that death does not represent the end. There is life after death. Even if a gun is pulled on them, they are not afraid. They know that they will live somewhere. They do not feel bad at funerals, but kind of rejoice at them.

To people who have been mortally afraid of death all their lives, it is as if God has sent this experience to them because of the way they felt about death. Their parents could at best comfort them, whereas the Lord showed them.

Persons who have died no longer use sleeping and forgetting as models of death. They choose analogies which portray death as a transition from one state to another, or as an entry into a higher state of consciousness (*altered states of consciousness*). They compare death to a homecoming, awakening, graduating and to an escape from a jail. Death is for them now a graduation from one thing to another, like from grammar school to high school to college.

Not a single NDEr has painted the mythological picture of what lies hereafter. No one has described the heaven of pearly gates, golden streets and winged, harp-playing angels, nor a hell of flames and demons with pitchforks. The reward-and-punishment model is abandoned. The subjects find to their amazement that when their most apparently awful and sinful deeds are made manifest, the being of light responds not with rage and anger, but with understanding and even with humor.

The new model of the world beyond does not feature unilateral judgement, but rather cooperative development towards the ultimate end of self-realization. Development of the soul, especially in the spiritual faculties of love and knowledge, does not stop at death. It continues on the other side, perhaps eternally.

### 1.2.15  Corroboration

The evidence from other sources corroborates much of what the subjects (NDErs) experienced. The attending doctors are baffled as to how their patients could have watched events or heard conversations while they were "dead". So are their near relatives. But these corroborations do not constitute proof.

# 1.3   Out-of-Body Experience (OBE)

An out-of-body experience (OBE) is a phenomenon in which a person perceives the world from a location outside their physical body. An OBE is a form of autoscopy (literally "seeing self"), although this term is more commonly used to refer to the pathological condition of seeing a second self.

The term out-of-body experience was introduced in 1943 by G. N. M. Tyrrell in his book Apparitions, and was adopted by researchers such as Celia Green, and Robert Monroe, as an alternative to belief-centric labels such as "astral projection" or "spirit walking". OBEs can be induced by traumatic brain injuries, sensory deprivation, near-death experiences, dissociative and psychedelic drugs, dehydration, sleep disorders, dreaming, and electrical stimulation of the brain, among other causes. It can also be deliberately induced by some. One in ten people has an OBE once, or more commonly, several times in their life.

Psychologists and neuroscientists regard OBEs as dissociative experiences occurring along different psychological and neurological factors.

### 1.3.1   Spontaneous OBEs

**(i) Sleep Paralysis**

Those experiencing OBEs sometimes report (among other types of immediate and spontaneous experience) a preceding and initiating lucid-dream state. In many cases, people who claim to have had an OBE report being on the verge of sleep, or being already asleep shortly before the experience. A large percentage of these cases refer to situations where the sleep was not particularly deep (due to illness, noises in other rooms, emotional stress, exhaustion from overworking, frequent re-awakening, etc.). In most of these cases subjects perceive themselves as being awake; about half of them note a feeling of sleep paralysis.

## (ii) Near-death experiences

Another form of spontaneous OBE is the near-death experience (NDE). Some subjects report having had an OBE at times of severe physical trauma such as near-drownings or major surgery. Near-death experiences may include subjective impressions of being outside the physical body, sometimes visions of deceased relatives and religious figures, and transcendence of ego and spatiotemporal boundaries. The experience typically includes such factors as: a sense of being dead; a feeling of peace and painlessness; hearing of various non-physical sounds, an out-of-body experience; a tunnel experience (the sense of moving up or through a narrow passageway); encountering "beings of light" and a God-like figure or similar entities; being given a "life review", and a reluctance to return to life.

## (iii) Resulting from Extreme Physical Effort

Along the same lines as an NDE, extreme physical effort during activities such as high-altitude climbing and marathon running can induce OBEs. A sense of bilocation may be experienced, with both ground and air-based perspectives being experienced simultaneously.

### 1.3.2   Induced OBEs

### (i) Chemical

OBEs can be induced by hallucinogens (particularly dissociative) such as psilocybin, ketamine, DMT, MDA, and LSD.

### (ii) Mental Induction

Falling asleep physically without losing awareness. The "Mind Awake, Body Asleep" state is widely suggested as a cause of OBEs, voluntary and otherwise. Thomas Edison used this state to tackle problems while working on his inventions. He would rest a silver dollar on his head while sitting with a metal bucket in a chair. As he drifted off, the coin would noisily fall into the bucket, restoring some of his alertness. OBE pioneer Sylvan Muldoon more simply used a forearm held perpendicular in bed as the falling object. Salvador Dalí was said to use a similar "paranoiac-critical" method to gain odd visions which inspired his paintings. Deliberately teetering between awake and asleep states is known to cause spontaneous trance episodes at the onset of sleep which are ultimately helpful when attempting to induce an OBE. By moving deeper and deeper into relaxation, one eventually encounters a "slipping" feeling if the mind is still alert. This slipping is reported to feel like leaving the physical body. Some consider progressive muscle relaxation as an active form of sensory deprivation.

## 1.4   Distressing Near-Death Experiences

The great majority of near-death experiences (NDEs) reported publicly have been described as pleasant, even glorious. Almost unnoticed in the euphoria about them has been the sobering fact that not all NDEs are so affirming. Some of these may be distressing or unpleasant too; which will be discussed in the following:

Few people are forthcoming about such an event; they hide; they disappear when asked for information; if in-patient, they are likely to withdraw; they are under great stress. What do their physicians need to know to deal with these experiences?

## 1.5   Types of Distressing Near-Death Experiences

Three types of distressing NDEs have been documented in this article:

(i) inverse NDE, void NDE, and hellish NDE.

The brief descriptions below illustrate these types.

### 1.5.1   Inverse NDE

In some NDEs, the experiences perceived as hostile or threatening. A man thrown from his horse found himself floating at treetop height, watching emergency medical technicians working over his body. "No! No! This isn't right!" He screamed, "Put me back!" but they did not hear him. Next he was shouting through darkness toward a bright light, flashing past shadowy people who seemed to be deceased family members waiting. He was panic-stricken by the bizarre scenario and his inability to affect what was happening.

A woman in childbirth felt her spirit separate from her body and fly into space at tremendous speed, then saw a small ball of light rushing toward her: "It became bigger and bigger as it came toward me. I realized that we were on a collision course, and it terrified me. I saw the blinding white light come right to me and engulf me."

A woman collapsed from hyperthermia and began re-experiencing her entire life: "I was filled with such sadness and experienced a great deal of depression."

### 1.5.2    The Void NDE

An NDE of the "void" is a metaphysical encounter with a perceived vast emptiness, often a devastating scenario of loneliness, isolation, sometimes annihilation. A woman in childbirth found herself abruptly flying over the hospital and into deep, empty space. A group of circular entities informed her that she never existed, that she had been allowed to imagine her life but it was a joke; she was not real. She argued with facts about her life and descriptions of Earth. "No," they said, "none of that had ever been real; this is all there was." She was left alone in space.

Another woman in childbirth felt herself floating on water, but at a certain point, "It was no longer a peaceful feeling; it had become pure hell. I had become a light out in the heavens, and I was screaming, but no sound was going forth. It was worse than any nightmare. I was spinning around, and I realized that this was eternity; this was what forever was going to be. I felt the loneliness, the emptiness of space, the vastness of the universe, except for me, a mere ball of light, screaming."

A woman who attempted suicide felt herself sucked into a void: "I was being drawn into this dark tunnel, or void. "I was not aware of my body as I know it. I was terrified. I felt terror. I had expected nothingness; I expected the big sleep; I expected oblivion; and I found now that I was going to another plane, and it frightened me. I wanted nothingness, but this force was pulling me somewhere I didn't want to go, and I never got beyond the fog."

A man who was attacked by a hitchhiker felt himself rise out of his body: "I suddenly was surrounded by total blackness, floating in nothing but black space, with no up, no down, left, or right. What seemed like an eternity went by. I fully lived it in this misery. I was only allowed to think and reflect."

### 1.5.3    Hellish NDE

Overtly hellish experiences may be the least common type of distressing NDE. A man in heart-failure felt himself falling into the depths of the Earth. At the bottom was a set of high, rusty gates, which he perceived as the gates of hell. Panic-stricken, he managed to scramble back up to daylight.

A woman was being escorted through a frighteningly desolate landscape and saw a group of wandering spirits. They looked lost and in pain, but her guide indicated she was not allowed to help them.

An atheistic university professor with an intestinal rupture experienced being maliciously pinched, then torn apart by malevolent beings.

A woman who hemorrhaged from a ruptured Fallopian tube reported an NDE involving "horrific beings with gray gelatinous appendages grasping and clawing at me. The sounds of their guttural moaning and the indescribable stench still remain forty-one years later. There was no benign Being of Light, no life video, nothing beautiful or pleasant."

A woman who attempted suicide felt her body sliding downward in a cold, dark, watery environment: "When I reached the bottom, it resembled the entrance to a cave, with what looked like webs hanging. I heard cries, wails, moans, and the gnashing of teeth. I saw these beings that resembled humans, with the shape of a head and body, but they were ugly and grotesque. They were frightening and sounded like they were tormented, in agony."

## 1.6 Three Types of Response in Distressing NDEs

These NDEs are traumatic in their realness, their rupturing the sense of worldly reality, and the power of the questions they raise. Three common responses cut across all experience types: the turnaround, reductionism, and the long haul.

### 1.6.1 The Turnaround: "I needed that"

A classic response to profound spiritual experience is conversion, not necessarily changing one's religion but in the original sense of meaning "to turn around." The terrifying NDE is interpreted as a warning about unwise or wrong behaviors, and to turn one's life around: "I was being shown that I had to shape up or ship out, one or the other. In other words, 'get your act together,' and I did just that."

Movement toward a dogmatic religious community is common in this group. Clinical social worker Kimberly Clark Sharp observed, "All the people I know who have had negative experiences have become Bible-based Christians. They might express it in various sects. But they all feel that they have come back from an awful situation and have a second chance."

Fear may remain a powerful influence, but a strict theology may offer a way out. The atheistic professor above who experienced being maliciously pinched, then torn apart by malevolent beings left his university and attended seminary. Others also reported newfound devotion, "I've stopped drugs, moved back to Florida, and now I'm in Bible college. I used to have a casual attitude toward death, but now I actually fear it more. So yes, it was a warning. I was permitted another chance to change my behavior on earth. I've taken my fear of death and given it to the scriptures." Since then, I have dedicated my life to the highest God Jehovah, and I spend 60 hours a month speaking and teaching about 'the Creator of Heaven and earth and all living creatures'. I'm not worried now about when I die, because now I know that God has promised us something far more."

### 1.6.2   Reductionism: "It was only …"

As a response to a distressing experience, reductionism has been described as the "defence [that] allows one to repudiate the meaning of an event which does not fit into a safe category" and to "treat the event as if it did not matter." (Reductionism is any of several related philosophical ideas regarding the associations between phenomena which can be described in terms of other simpler or more fundamental phenomena. It is also described as an intellectual and philosophical position that interprets a complex system as the sum of its parts).

A woman whose anaphylactic reaction precipitated an NDE with both loving and frightening elements concluded, "There are actual rational explanations for what I experienced. The brain, under stress, releases natural opiates that stop pain and fear. Lack of oxygen disrupts the normal activity of the visual cortex. Too much neural activity in the dying brain causes stripes of activity. Our eyes, even closed, interpret those stripes of activity as the sensation of moving forward in a tunnel. There are more brain cells concentrated in the middle of the cortex than on the edges so as we get closer to death, the brain interprets all those dense cells with their crazy activity as a bright light in the middle of our visual field. It's all very scientific."

Her conclusion is that, based on the scientific evidence, the experience had no metaphysical meaning. Any lingering anxieties will go unaddressed.

A woman who had a terrifying experience during childbirth likewise dismissed the reality of the experience: "Perhaps it was the effect of the ether and not an NDE." A woman attacked by a lion dismissed the memory of her NDE as hallucinatory: "I often wonder if, in the shock of the attack, my mind played tricks on me, and that I may have just been unconscious and my brain deprived of oxygen."

A man who for many years had spoken publicly about his radiant NDE had a second experience, in which he felt attacked by gigantic, sinister, threatening geometric forms, leaving him with a deep-seated pessimism and terror of dying. Learning that drug-induced hallucinations include geometric forms, he concluded that his second NDE was "only a drug reaction." This may be an appropriate conclusion clinically, but the experience remains. Reductionism provides a temporary buffer to mask questions and anxieties, but does nothing to resolve them.

### 1.6.3 The Long Haul: "What did I do?"

Other experiencers have difficulty comprehending or integrating terrifying NDEs. These people, years later, still struggle with the existential implications of the NDE, "I had an experience which has remained with me for 29 years. It has left a horror in my mind and I have never spoken about it until now." And, "After all these years, the nightmare remains vivid in my mind." "For some reason, (31 years later) all the memories are back and vivid. It's like living it all over again, and I don't want to. I thought I had it all resolved and in its place, but I'm having a really bad time trying to put it away this time."

Also, "For the next 50 years, I would try to repress the memory of the black, threatening experience, because it felt so real that it continued to be frightening, no matter how old I got." And, "I've been married for 33 years and I do not even discuss the experience with my husband. Yet it is as clear to me today as it was when it happened." Additionally, "I just buried the whole thing as deeply as possible, got very busy in civic affairs, politics. It seems pretty clear to me now, though the specifics aren't in place, that there's some core issues that still need dealing with."

"I see this vision as flashbacks constantly. I cannot get this out of my head. I still see it in my mind from my own eyes. It has been two years, yet I have never talked about it. My husband does not even know. I want to put this behind me, but am unable to do so."

This group is often articulate people haunted by the existential dimension of their NDE, searching for a cognitively and emotionally grounding explanation. They find a literal reading of the event intellectually unacceptable, but reductionist explanations only assign a cause without addressing meaning. They struggle to make sense of the distressing NDE without destroying them (and their trust in the workings of the world) in the process.

More than others, these experiencers enter psychotherapy, some for many years, though without data, this may indicate nothing other than openness and financial means. Too often physicians prescribe medications to mask questioning and dismiss the NDE as fanciful or pathological; therapists will not address the matter or leave the client feeling blamed or romanticize spirituality and cannot deal with its dark side; and clergy have no idea what to say or reject the experience outright.

The religious element of their NDE is often an absence:

"I was filled with a sense of absolute terror and of being past the help of anyone, even God."

"I looked around me. Consciously searching for. God or some other angelic creature, but I was alone."

"I expected the Lord to be there, but He wasn't. I called on God and He wasn't there. That's what scared me."

Overwhelmingly, their questions include some variant of "What did I do to deserve this?" or "What are the rules, if the rules I lived by don't work?" Not for a long time, if ever, do they lose their fear of death." The man above attacked by a hitchhiker still struggled with the aftermath, "I've pondered if I was in that hell, will I go back on my death? Was I sent there for something perhaps I'll do in the future, or something I did in the past?. I don't believe in a hell, but it was such a strong experience, there is always that underlying uncertainty and trouble and fear."

## 1.7 Post-Traumatic Growth

The psychological literature on post-traumatic growth did not exist in the early years of study of distressing NDEs, so that aspect of response remains underreported. As a growing number of studies make clear, even the most devastating life event, "like the grit that creates the oyster, is often what propels people to become more-true to themselves, take on new challenges, and view life from a wider perspective." This is a promising and as yet underdeveloped approach for clinicians working with those who report struggling after a distressing NDE.

## 1.8 Seven Things to know about Distressing Near-Death Experiences

(i) Distressing NDEs occur under the same wide range of circumstances and feature most of the same elements as pleasant NDEs. What differs is the emotional tone, which ranges from fear through terror to, in some cases, guilt or despair. The reports typically lack two elements common in pleasant NDEs: a positive emotional tone and loss of the fear of death.

(ii) A notorious reluctance to report a distressing NDE may lead to long-lasting trauma for individuals as well as limiting the data on occurrence. A literature review covering thirty years of research concludes that as many as one in five NDEs may be predominantly distressing.

(iii) The etiology(the scientific study of the causes of disease) of all such events remains unknown. Despite decades of clinical studies, none so far adequately explains either the cause or function of NDEs. Further, NDEs cross so many clinical circumstances and demographic bases, there is no way to predict who will have what type of NDE. No evidence supports the conventional assumption that "good" people get pleasant NDEs and "bad" people have distressing ones. Saints have reported extremely disturbing NDEs, while felons and suicide attempters have encountered bliss.

(iv)   Pleasant NDEs tend to convey universal messages of compassion that cross religious and philosophical systems. Distressing NDEs typically have less focused messages but follow the ancient shamanic pattern of suffering/death/ resurrection, which in less metaphoric terms can be read as an invitation to self-examination, disarrangement of core beliefs, and rebuilding. In practical terms, a common interpretation of a distressing NDE is that it is a message to turn one's life around.

(v)    description of any NDE is shaped by the experiencer's pre-existing mental categories and vocabulary. As example, although the archetype of a benevolent guide is common in NDEs, individuals typically identify the presence according to their own cultural vocabulary. Any report identifying an archetypal individual by name is a perception that may or may not be factually true but cannot be confirmed as such. Understandably, it is facts like these which religious groups and materialists alike may find troubling. Secular Westerners often believe an NDE indicates a psychotic episode.

(vi)   The primary effect of many NDEs is a powerful and enduring awareness that the physical world is not the full extent of reality. Because this perception runs so deeply counter to Western materialism, and conversely because its implications affect some dogmatic theological teachings, the new conviction commonly overturns experiencers' personal life and social relationships abruptly and permanently.

(vii)  A major challenge for physicians and other scientists dealing with reports of near-death experience is to manage this intrusion of non-materialist religious and philosophical language and understandings into the hard data of clinical thinking. Curiously, it is at the extremes of religious fundamentalism and material scientism that one finds literalism an issue. For fundamentalists, the accounts are believed to be literally, physically actual; for convinced materialists, they must be dismissed as lunacy because a literal, physical actuality is impossible and no alternative concept is acceptable.

## 1.9    NDEs of the Children

Very young children, as soon as they are able to speak, have reported NDEs they had as infants, or even in the process of being born. NDEs of children are different from the family teachings of death, and their experiences are structured similar to the adult ones. In the OBEs, they see themselves as adults and not as baby spirits. But some have also seen their living playmates in their NDE. A researcher, who herself had three NDEs in 1977, posits that 'children who had near-death episodes are remodeled, rewired, reconfigured and are the refined version of the original.' Children who have experienced NDEs display precocious wisdom and certainty about life after death. Frightening childhood NDEs are rare in the literature, but a few have been reported. Such experiences lead to nightmares, restlessness, and prolonged anxiety among the children. These distressing experiences begin or end with a positive note. Near death research is an area where subject matter cannot be observed directly and so it is difficult to do quality research. Children's narration of NDEs is particularly valuable and enlightening because they report accurately what they experience without undue apprehension over the rational interpretation of their experiences.

## 1.10    NDEs of the Blind

A researcher's study of NDEs among blind persons sought corroborative evidence regarding the authenticity of their unusual experience. He claimed that even those blind from birth reported classic NDEs and the great majority of those claimed to see during their NDEs-eyeless vision. A few of them reported visually-based knowledge, whose truthfulness was independently verified, which could not have been acquired by ordinary means. In another study of blind people's NDEs, 80% claimed some visual perceptions during the NDE or OBE encounters. It was also noticed that sometimes the initial onset of visual perceptions of the physical world was disorienting and even distressing to the blind. Near-death researchers who are enthusiastic about cases of veridical (truthful) paranormal perception generally overlook hallucinatory NDEs, and there is clear evidence that NDErs have sometimes false perceptions of physical world. The over-enthusiasm of such passionate survival researchers may have been a defence against the reductionist stance of the last century.

## 1.11  Implications of Near-Death Experiences (NDEs)

"Near-death experiences" include phenomena that challenge materialist reductionism, such as enhanced mentation (mental activity) and memory during cerebral impairment, accurate perceptions from a perspective outside the body, and reported visions of deceased persons, including those not previously known to the deceased. Complex consciousness, including cognition, perception, and memory, under conditions such as cardiac arrest and general anesthesia, when it cannot be associated with normal brain function, requires a revised analysis of NDE, which cannot be explained by the classical physics but rather of 21st-century's **quantum physics** that includes **consciousness** in its conceptual formulation. Classical physics (Newtonian physics), anchored in materialist reductionism, offered adequate descriptions of everyday mechanics but ultimately proved insufficient for describing the mechanics of extremely high speeds or small sizes, and was supplemented by quantum physics. Materialist psychology, modeled on the reductionism of classical physics, likewise offered adequate descriptions of everyday mental functioning but ultimately proved insufficient for describing mentation under extreme conditions, such as the continuation of mental function when the brain is inactive or impaired, such as occurs near death.

# CHAPTER 2

# LIFE AFTER DEATH: A RELIGIOUS PERSPECTIVE

## 2.1    What happens after Death?

What happens after death? No one knows the answer with certainty. You may find some answers, but you will not be sure whether they are right. Some spiritual gurus try to answer it. Each speaks for about half an hour or so. They go round and round the subject, but are not forthright. Either they do not know or they are trying to avoid a definitive answer. Following answer might provide a unique perspective on the subject in contemporary terms, which is a close approximation to the traditional schools of **Advaita and Vishishtadvaita**.

Death is a mystery, and the afterlife is still a greater mystery. No one really knows what happens to a being or a soul after death. Each religion answers this question in its own ways. They disagree rather than agree on the particulars, processes, and possibilities. There are as many theories and descriptions as there are religions, schools of philosophy and spiritual traditions.

**Christians** believe that if you accept Jesus Christ as your savior, upon death you will enter the heaven of God and live in His Company. Otherwise, you will be condemned to an eternal hell.

**Muslims** also believe in God´s heaven, but it is a different heaven where only believers of Allah can enter, and the rest will go to hell.

The **Buddhists** believe in the existence of multiple heavens and hells. According to them, upon death a person enters one or more of the heavenly or hellish worlds, depending upon the state of his mind at the time of death. For them, afterlife in any of those worlds is a distraction for the mortal beings, which delays their liberation and prolongs their suffering.

**Hinduism** also believes in multiple worlds of light and darkness. However, the predominant belief is that upon death the souls go to either the eternal world of Brahman, if they achieve liberation, or the ancestral world if they have not resolved their karma. The ancestral world is a temporary world. The transmigrating souls stay there until their karmas are exhausted and return to earth to take another birth.

One has numerous new-age movements, each with its own version of what happens to a soul upon death. Some even believe in the existence of alien planets and extra-terrestrial worlds, to which souls would go upon death and continue their existence.

Some **teacher-traditions in India** and elsewhere suggest that souls will enter astral worlds upon death, which are in many ways said to be similar to our world but are subtle, where the departed souls enjoy greater freedom and flexibility in manifesting their desires and wishes. Finally, we have **atheists** who think that heaven and hell are figments of imagination, and death is true liberation.

Thus, you can see that there are numerous beliefs, opinions, and theories about life after death, and what happens to the souls after they depart from here.

## 2.2    Fate of Animals after Death

There is also no unanimity among the faiths about the fate of animals, and other creatures after they die. Some believe that all living beings possess souls and are in different stages of spiritual evolution. Hence, they too enter heaven or hell according to their deeds. Some believe that animals too have their animal heaven where they stay after death and return to the earth in a higher form. Others hold that birds, animals, and other creatures have no souls, and do not have any afterlife. For them, it is as if this world is some big Disneyland where the Big One has provided humans with numerous living and breathing toys for food, entertainment, and target practice.

## 2.3   Near-Death Experiences of Religious Persons

The near-death experiences which are recorded by many also do not provide a clear picture. Numerous studies show that people differ in the particulars of their near-death experiences. In other words, on the deathbed they all do not experience the same world or go through the same circumstances. Their experiences closely match their state of consciousness, or they faith, values and beliefs.

For example, in a near-death experience, a **Hindu** is more likely to see a spiritual teacher (Guru) or a heaven or hell as described in the epics and Puranas, whereas a **Christian** might see Jesus-like figure or an angel walking towards him in a bright light. Similarly, Buddhists and Muslims might see different worlds and go through different experiences according to their beliefs. In all such cases, it is their minds that seem to be drawing them into the worlds that match their beliefs, knowledge, and awareness.

## 2.4   Everything is a Projection: Maya

Logically speaking, it appears that what people might experience in the last stages of their lives or in their afterlives is shaped largely by the quality and nature of their consciousness. It is a projection of their consciousness which creates the reality and provides them with the experience. Since consciousness is unique to each person and to each case, the experience of reality will also be different to each person. It is more likely that if the same person undergoes two near-death experiences at two stages in his life, one in the young age and the second in the old age, his two experiences may not entirely be the same.

The diversity of experience in the phenomenal world is the common theme of life in all forms and stages. It holds true for every living being upon earth. You can see that nothing in creation is fixed. Everything moves and changes. The impermanence and flexibility of the world are why we experience our lives uniquely and differently. It is also reason enough for us to respect life, to be tolerant, and let each soul live the life. We may all go through identical situations, but they leave different impressions in our minds and consciousness because we all do not perceive, think or know alike.

The reality, which is experienced by each soul upon earth, is its own projection. It is colored by its consciousness. Hence, although we all live in the same world and on the same planet, we experience different realities and live in different worlds. They are colored by our knowledge, awareness, desires, intentions, relationships, expectations, fears, hopes, religious and social backgrounds, and so on.

It gets even more bizarre as we enter our deeper consciousness. Whatever little similarities and common grounds that exist in the external world greatly disappear in the subtle worlds, where your consciousness is the sole architect of all that it creates and enjoys. You are literally the God of those worlds, or Ishvara, the lord. You are the subject and the object of what happens there. You are the knower and the known. You are the Brahman of that universe, who cannot be perceived but who makes that perception possible.

For example, take your own dream world. Each time you dream, you enter a different world. Your two dreams will never be the same. No two people will ever dream the same dream. Each dream is a world in itself, which is shaped by your consciousness and its essential nature. Your thoughts, hopes, fears, desires, attachments, expectations, memories, previous actions, knowledge, and imagination provide the bricks and mortar for those creations you manifest in your dreams. The same happens when you meditate and visualize. Even if you practice a guided meditation, what you create in your mind will be unique.

## 2.5    Afterlife is also a Projection of the Self only

The same process is repeated when a person dies. When a soul or the consciousness is released from the body and enters the dimensions of higher realms, it begins to project its own reality and creates its own world according to the state of mind and purity of consciousness. If the soul is completely pure, as in the case of liberated beings, it projects an infinite reality, in which nothing exists except itself. It becomes the sum of all, the totality of all, the absolute perfection, the singular constant that is indestructible, unchanging, eternal, and indivisible, without a second.

If it has impurities, as in case of transmigrating souls, the world that it creates will be limited by its own impurities, the state of mind, predominant desires, habitual thoughts, latent impressions, suppressed fears, and uncontrollable longings. It will still be the Lord of that limited, grayish world, in which it will manifest its reality according to its likes and dislikes but the creation will not be as majestic or expansive as that of the pure Self. It lives in it, and experiences pleasure and pain and other dualities of life according to its accumulated karma.

In this regard, the following points are worth considering:

- Souls are eternal, indestructible, indivisible and infinite. However, in Samsara they are subject to Maya, the power of Nature.

- Pure souls that are liberated exist in a state of infinity after departing from here. They project infinite universes within themselves and possess no other awareness, nor do they project any reality that leads to experience of duality and division.

- Impure souls, which are bound to Nature and clouded by delusion and ignorance due to

Maya, project a mixed reality of light and darkness according to their predominant modes and desires. Because of delusion, they take those worlds for real and remain deluded. Their delusion continues even in afterlife, where they accept the worlds which they project as real and become involved with them.

Thus, the experience of afterlife is unique to each soul and largely shaped by its purity and state of consciousness. Upon departing from here each embodied soul projects its own reality, creates its own world or worlds in the subtle realms, according to the predominant gunas, beliefs, desires, and attachments. It projects subtle copies of the beings and objects to which it is attached, and creates a world which will be a close approximation to the nature of its surviving consciousness. Having projected the world or worlds, it enjoys them as the lord and witness. If the consciousness is purer, it projects purer and brighter worlds and inhabits them as their lord. If the consciousness is dark and clouded, it projects similar worlds and remains deluded by them.

## 2.6    What you do now, determines how you live there

Neither this world nor the next world is real. Both are projections of the Self which has a universal dimension in its purest state and a limited potency in bound state. In both situations, due to Maya the Self takes its creations or projections for real and identifies itself with them. The nature of its projections and involvement depend very much upon what it experiences here and what it accumulates, just as your dream world and deep sleep experiences are closely related to what you experience in your wakeful state.

For example, if you spend most of the time in the company of bad people, you will have trouble sleeping peacefully. The same happens in life too. If you do not regulate your life upon earth or if you indulge in indiscriminate actions, you will have a troublesome afterlife. If you do not purify your mind and body, or allow negative qualities to prevail, in your afterlife you will involve yourself with darker and fearsome worlds and subject yourself to painful agony.

## 2.7 You are the Court, the Judge, the Witness, and the Defendant

Here are a few points that are worth remembering:

- Whatever is here or hereafter, you are the one who manifest your life and create your world.

  There is no one to punish you or reward you in the next life. You do it yourself with the projection of your consciousness.

- You are the lord and the master of the universe that you create, and the worlds which you inhabit.

- You pervade those worlds, which you create in different realms or planes of existence, and enter them too as its sole inhabitant.

- Everything that manifests in those worlds is your projection and you only. You appear in numerous forms and with numerous identities to create the illusion of diversity.


Therefore, when you think of death, know that your existence in the next world will be similar to what your mind projects now. Whether you want to keep it pure or clouded, it is up to you.

You are the source of both life and death. Even in delusion, you do not cease to create and manifest, just as the sun does not cease to radiate life even when it is covered by clouds. Whether it is here or in the next world, you are always the same eternal Self. What changes or keeps changing is the reality that you project.

To conclude, *the mind is the tool of the CONSCIOUSNESS (with capital letters) to manifest Itself in us, and to let us see It in all.* Veiled in beasts and low natured humans, fully manifested in saints, Mahatmas and Avatars, but present in all and everywhere, for your benefit and the benefit of the whole, let your mind be a clear crystal.

## 2.8 What exactly happens after Death according to Hinduism?

Around the world, what happens after death can be divided into two schools: Those who believe you live only once and those who believe you live multiple lives.

We can either be reborn (punar-janma) and experience life once again, or be liberated (moksha) from the cycle of rebirth (samsara). However, the answer is a bit more complex if we see it geographically and historically.

Those who believe you live only once have broadly three schools—(i) those who believe death is the end, nothing else after that; (ii) those who believe after death you go to the land of the dead and stay in this afterlife forever; and (iii) those who believe after death you go to either heaven, where you enjoy the rest of eternity, or to hell, where you suffer for all eternity (or maybe until you have been adequately punished and are ready to join the rest in heaven).

Those who believe in rebirth believe you keep coming back from the land of the dead (pitṛ-loka) to the land of the living (bhu-loka) until you learn the ultimate lesson after which you no longer feel the need for a body. There are variations on this, where you are punished for various crimes in hell (Naraka-loka) before you are ready to be reborn, or where you enjoy heaven (swarga-loka), until it is time for your return to earth once again.

Ancient Egyptians built pyramids because they believed in an eternal afterlife. Ancient Chinese, before Buddhism introduced the idea of rebirth, have always believed in the land of ancestors that one has to go to after death. Even today, there are rituals where you offer paper money to ancestors to spend in the land of the dead, from whence there is no return.

While rebirth and re-death (punar-mrityu) are seen as inevitable, **Hindus** have also believed in the concept of immortality (amrita). The devas who live in the sky and the asuras who live under the earth, fight over this nectar, as do birds (Garuda) and snakes (Naga). We hear that asuras have Sanjivani Vidya, by which they can resurrect the dead. This is used by Jayanta to bring Shukra back to life. We hear in the Mahabharata that the serpents have Naga-mani, or serpent jewel, that can bring back the dead to life; this is used to bring Arjuna back to life after he is shot dead by Babruvahana.

Historically, in the Vedas, we do not find a clear reference to rebirth. There is reference to how our body, after it dies, returns to nature, just like the primordial purusha: so his eye becomes the sun, his breath becomes the wind. There is reference to something that outlives death: atman, jiva, manas, prana. There is reference to a happy land of ancestors and gods (swarga) and to the painful land below the three heavens (Naraka). There is reference to feeding the ancestors (pitr or shrādha). But the idea of rebirth as we know it today is not yet formed.

The idea of rebirth evolves in the Upanishads and fully expressed in the Puranas. While the Vedic householders believed performance of yagna and worldly duties (dharma) took one to heaven, the Vedic hermits spoke of the karma theory, of immortality, of uniting the individual self (atma, jiva-atma) with the cosmic self (brahman, param-atma) through meditation (dhyana), austerities (Tapasya) and various social, mental, and physical exercise (yoga).

What we find are two options merging: return to this world in another form, or escape to another world. Hence, Hindu rituals are a combination of fire (for escape) and water (for rebirth). There are even communities that choose burial. There are communities that feed ancestors in rituals (shrādha) and promise to help their rebirth. In this ritual, we focus on the relationship of food (anna) and flesh (anna-kosha), and how the dead yearn to return to the land of the living, have flesh and consume food, while striving for liberation.

Then there is the concept of voluntary renouncing the body (samadhi), which rationalists argue is actually self-termination of life after fulfilling worldly duties. For example, Lord Rama in the Ramayana walks into the river Sarayu and does not rise again after he passes on his kingdom to his children. Likewise, Pandavas walk away into mountains after passing on their kingdom to the next generation. Is this suicide? The faithful see it as merging of jiva-atma with param-atma voluntarily by yogis. The sceptics disagree.

Now since suicide is a sin in Christianity, until recently in India, in keeping with its colonial legacy, attempting suicide was a crime. However, Indians have had a mature relationship with death. It is perfectly fine to voluntarily give up life, after completing all worldly duties, with permission of those of family. This is controversial today, but a common theme in the Puranas. Hence, the concept of Sanyasa-ashrama, the final stage of life, when you walk away from worldly duties and focus on the divine.

## 2.9   Near-Death Experience, as mentioned in Garuda Purana

### 2.9.1   Garuda Purana

The Garuda Purana is one of 18 Mahapurana texts in Hinduism. It is a part of Vaishnavism literature corpus, primarily centering around Hindu god Vishnu. It is composed in Sanskrit. The earliest version of the text may have been composed in the first millennium CE, but it was likely expanded and changed over a long period of time.

The Garuda Purana text is known in many versions, contains 15000+ verses. Its chapters encyclopedically deal with a highly diverse collection of topics. The text contains cosmology, mythology, relationship between gods, ethics, good versus evil, various schools of Hindu philosophies, the theory of Yoga, the theory of "heaven and hell" with "karma and rebirth", ancestral rites and soteriology, rivers and geography, types of minerals and stones, testing methods for gems for their quality, listing of plants and herbs, various diseases and their symptoms, various medicines, aphrodisiacs, prophylactics, Hindu calendar and its basis, astronomy, moon, planets, astrology, architecture, building home, essential features of a Hindu temple, rites of passage, charity and gift making, economy, thrift, duties of a king, politics, state officials and their roles and how to appoint them, genre of literature, rules of grammar, and other topics. The final chapters discuss how to practice Yoga (Samkhya and Advaita types), personal development and the benefits of self-knowledge.

The text was composed sometime in the first millennium of the common era, but it was likely compiled and changed over a long period of time. The first version of the text was written between the fourth century CE and the eleventh century. The text is likely from about 900 CE, given that it includes chapters on Yoga and Tantra techniques that likely developed later. Other scholars suggest that the earliest core of the text may be from the first centuries of the common era, and additional chapters were added thereafter through the sixth century or later. The version of the Garuda Purana that survives into the modern era, is likely from 800 to 1000 CE, with sections added in the 2nd millennium.

The write up below provides a gist of the great teachings in the Garuda Purana:

- What Happens After Death?

- What is death?

- Is there life after death?

- Is death painful?

- What happens after death?

- How does rebirth happen?

- Where do we go after death?

These kind of questions related to the most feared event that ends our life always fill our mind, especially when any of our near or dear ones die.

A few hours before an individual dies, his/her feet turn cold. When the actual time to depart arrives, it is said that Yama, the God of death appears to guide the soul.

### 2.9.2   The Astral Cord

According to the Garuda Purana, a person who is about to die cannot speak even if he wants to. At the last moment, divine vision arises in him and he begins to understand the whole world as one. Death severs the astral cord, which is the connection of the soul to the body. Once this cord is cut, the soul becomes free of the body and moves up and out of the body. If the soul is attached to the physical body it occupied for this lifetime, it refuses to leave and tries to get into the body and move it and stay in it. We may observe this as a very subtle or slight movement of the face, hand or leg after the person has died. The soul is unable to accept that it is dead. There is still a feeling of being alive. Since the astral cord has been severed, the soul cannot stay here and is pushed upwards and out of the body. There is a pull from above … a magnetic pull to go up.

### 2.9.3   End of the Physical Body

At this stage the soul hears many voices, all at the same time. These are the thoughts of all the individuals present in the room. The soul on its part talks to his loved ones like he always did and shouts out "I am not dead"! ! But alas, nobody hears him…

Slowly and steadily the soul realizes that it is dead and there is no way back. At this stage, the soul is floating at approximately twelve feet at the height of the ceiling, seeing and hearing everything happening around.

Generally the soul floats around the body till it is cremated. So, the next time if you see a body being carried for cremation, be informed that the soul is also part of the procession seeing, hearing and witnessing everything and everyone.

### 2.9.4   Detachment from the Body

Once the cremation is complete, the soul is convinced that. the main essence of its survival on earth is lost and the body it occupied for so many years has merged into the five elements. The soul experiences complete freedom, the boundaries it had while being in the body are gone and it can travel anywhere by mere thought.

For seven days the soul moves about its places of interest like its favorite joint, morning walk garden, office, etc. If the soul is possessive of his money, it will just stay near his cupboard, or if he is possessive of his children, it will just be in their room, clinging on to them. By the end of the seventh day, the soul says 'bye' to his family and moves further upwards to the periphery of the earth plane to cross over to the other side.

### 2.9.5　The Tunnel

It is said that there is a big tunnel here which it has to cross before reaching the astral plane. Hence its said that the first twelve days after death are extremely crucial. We have to carry out the rituals correctly and pray and ask forgiveness from the soul, so that it does not carry negative emotions like hurt, hatred, anger, etc at least from the near and dear ones. All the rituals, prayers and positive energy act like food for the soul which will help it in its onward journey. At the end of the tunnel is a huge bright light signifying the entry into the astral world.

### 2.9.6　Meeting the Ancestors

On the 11th and 12th day Hindus conduct homas (havans/yajnas) and prayers and rituals through which the soul is united with its ancestors, close friends, relatives and the guides. All the passed away ancestors welcome the soul to the upper plane and they greet and hug them exactly like we do here on seeing our family members after a long time. The soul then along with its guides are taken for a thorough life-review of the life just completed on earth in the presence of the 'Great Karmic Board.' It is here in the pure light that the whole past life is viewed!

### 2.9.7　Life-Review

There is no judge, there is no God here. The soul judges himself, the way he judged others in his lifetime. He asks for revenge for people who troubled him in that life, he experiences. guilt for all wrongdoings he did to people and asks for self-punishment to learn that lesson. Since the soul is not bound by the body and. the ego, the final judgment becomes the basis of the next lifetime. Based on this, a complete life structure is created by the soul himself, called the blue print. All the incidents to be faced, all problems to be faced, all challenges to be overcome are written in this agreement. In fact, the soul chooses all the minute details like age, person and circumstances for all incidents to be experienced.

**Example:** An individual had severe headache in his present birth, nothing helped him, no medicines, no way out. In a session of past life regression, he saw himself killing his neighbor in a previous birth by smashing his head with a huge stone. In the life-review, when he saw this he became very guilty and. asked for the same pain to be experienced by him by way of a never-ending headache in this life.

### 2.9.8  Blue Print

This is the way we judge ourselves and in guilt ask for punishment. The amount of guilt in the soul, decides the severity of the punishment and the level of suffering. Hence forgiveness is very vital. We must forgive and seek forgiveness! Clear your thoughts and emotions, as we carry them forward to the other side too. Once this review is done and our blue print for the next life is formed, then there is a cooling period.

### 2.9.9  The Re-birth

We are born depending on what we have asked for in the agreement. The cooling off period also depends on our urgency to evolve. We choose our parents and enter the mothers' womb either at the time of egg formation or during the 4–5th month or sometimes even at the last moment just before birth. The universe is so perfect, so beautifully designed that the time and. place of birth constitutes our horoscope, which actually is a blue print of this life. Most of us think that our stars are bad and we are unlucky but in actuality, they just mirror your agreement. Once we are reborn, for around 40 days, the baby remembers its past life and laughs and cries by itself without anyone forcing it to. The memory of the past life is completely cut after this and we experience life as though we did not exist in the past.

### 2.9.10   The Agreement Starts

It is here that we are completely on the earth plane and the contract comes into full effect. We then blame God/people for our difficult situations and. curse God for giving us such a difficult life. So, the next time before pointing to the Divine, understand that our circumstances are just helping us complete and honor our agreement, which is fully and completely written by us. Whatever we have asked for and pre-decided is exactly what we receive! Friends, relatives, foes, parents, spouses all have been selected by us in the blue print and come in our lives based on this agreement. They are just playing their parts and are merely actors in this film written, produced and directed by us!

### 2.9.11   Do the dead need healing/prayers/protection?

The dead always need serious healing and. prayers for a variety of reasons, the most important one being: To be free and not earthbound; that is stuck in the earth plane and unable to leave. There are many reasons for the soul to be earthbound like unfinished business, excessive grief, trauma on death, sudden death, fear of moving on to the astral plane, guilt, one of the most important being improper finishing of last rites and rituals. The soul feels it needs a little more time to wait and finish before moving on. This keeps them hovering on the earth plane. But the time is limited and it is very important that they cross over within twelve days to their astral plane of existence, as the entry to the astral world closes a few days after this.

**Recital of Garuda Purana** is a Hindu tradition which takes place whenever there is a death in the family till the completion of **13th day ceremony.**

Earth-bound spirits lead a very miserable existence as they are neither in their actual plane nor in a body to lead an earthly life. They may not be negative or harmful but they are stuck and miserable. Hence healing and prayers are of utmost importance during this period so that the departed soul crosses over to the designated astral plane peacefully. Prayers by the whole family are very vital to help the dead cross over. The protection of the soul to help it reach its destination in the astral world is achieved through prayers.

# CHAPTER 3

# STUDIES ON NEAR-DETH EXPERIENCES

## 3.1 Studies on Near-death Experiences (NDEs)

In a general classification of Near-death Experiences (NDEs), two factors have been introduced as the origin of these experiences. Some differentiate between theories that link NDE to physiological changes in the brain and theories which see NDEs as a psychological reaction to approaching death. The earlier studies have highlighted the uniqueness of NDE memories in the autobiographical memory, stating that NDE memories contain more sensory, emotional, and self-referential details in comparison with the memories of other real and imaginary events, or the memories of a coma or impaired consciousness following an acquired brain dysfunction without NDE. Near-death experiences occur in various situations, including cardiac arrest in MI (myocardial infarction) (clinical death), the shocks caused by the blood loss after delivery or in postoperative complications, septic or anaphylactic shocks, electrocution, the coma caused by traumatic brain injury, intracerebral hemorrhage or cerebral infarction, suicide attempts, near drowning or suffocation experiences, apnea (stopping of breathing for a short duration), and other cases where death is unavoidable. The occurrence of near-death experiences is increasing thanks to improved survival rates through modern medical techniques.

In a study conducted by Hashemi, et al. (2023), the results show that sharing and investigating this phenomenon may happen 5–10 years after the occurrence of the experience, which often prevents the accurate evaluation of physiological and pharmacological factors. In addition, the results of studies show that the prevalence of this phenomenon in the patients who have gone into cardiac arrest varies between 3.6 and 23%. Other retrospective studies have estimated that between 43 and 48% of adults, and 85% of children who have been affected by life-threatening illnesses may have experienced the NDE phenomenon.

The occurrence of these experiences leads to positive consequences in some NDEr such as a more altruistic life, higher spiritual growth, having interest in the meaning of life, fewer materialistic values, or a reduction in the fear of death. Their subjective nature and the lack of a clear framework for these experiences make the description and the interpretation of these experiences dependent on individual, cultural, or religious factors. Near-death experiences vary depending on the survivors' own cultural and religious background, and are almost always described based on the individual's religious beliefs. Most of the early studies on NDEs only depict positive emotions.

Some studies have also mentioned negative experiences in NDEs, including "hellish" ones, although it seems that some NDEr's may still be reluctant to share their experiences. Numerous quantitative and qualitative studies have been published on patients' experiences of this phenomenon. In the oldest study in this field, Raymond A. Moody compared the continental differences of experiencers. Combining research results allows qualitative studies to be conducted to reveal new insights or to identify whether subject saturation has occurred. In addition to qualitative evidence, the majority of studies have collected quantitative data on patients' experiences through structured questionnaires or interviews. The results of the researches that have been carried out since 1981 in the field of NDE indicate that the treatment staff, especially nurses and doctors, have little knowledge of these experiences, while this knowledge is necessary to identify the NDEr's and help them cope with their experiences. These experiences cause deep and lasting changes in patients' personalities, which highlights the necessity of helping these patients to properly understand and perceive the NDE phenomenon and integrate its consequences.

Due to the fact that different studies have reached different results and the results of these studies have not been certain, so it is necessary to search for a definite result for a correct understanding of this phenomenon. In the present study, the use of experts' opinions and the review of key journals, this systematic review can have a more comprehensive review of the relevant subject. Examining these experiences may pose challenges to the researchers of sciences such as psychology, parapsychology, psychiatry, medicine, philosophy of religion, and psychology of religion, each of which requires competent and well-reasoned answers. This systematic review reports a combination of the evidence related to patients' experiences- case reports, case series, and qualitative research- in order to achieve a comprehensive perception of patients' experiences. Considering the potential causes and the unpredictable aspect of this phenomenon, an overview of patients' experiences seems necessary.

This study focused on two specific review questions:

(i)  "What common experiences regarding the NDEr's accounts of NDE phenomena can be drawn from the results of the existing studies?", and

(ii)  "What broad knowledge can be gained from the NDEr's accounts of these common experiences?"

### 3.1.1  Types of Studies

In the current research, all case reports, case series, and qualitative research studies mentioning near-death experiences have been selected for entering. The eligible population included individuals who had experienced unavoidable death and NDE without any age, gender, race, or ethnicity restrictions.

Without any language restrictions, studies were searched in various journal dedicated to NDE and the Google data base.

Case Series and Case Reports checklist questions included 10 questions, respectively:

(i)  Were there clear criteria for inclusion in the case series?

(ii) Was the condition measured in a standard, reliable way for all participants included in the case series?

(iii) Were valid methods used for identification of the condition for all participants included in the case series?

(iv) Did the case series have consecutive inclusion of participants?

(v) Did the case series have complete inclusion of participants?

(vi) Was there clear reporting of the demographics of the participants in the study?

(vii) Was there clear reporting of clinical information of the participants?

(viii) Were the outcomes or follow-up results of cases clearly reported?

(ix) Was there clear reporting of the presenting site(s)/clinic(s) demographic information?, and

(x) Was statistical analysis appropriate?

The questions of the qualitative checklist included 10 questions:

(i) Is there congruity between the stated philosophical perspective and the research methodology?

(ii) Is there congruity between the research methodology and the research question or objectives?

(iii) Is there congruity between the research methodology and the methods used to collect data?

(iv) Is there congruity between the research methodology and the representation and analysis of data?

(v) Is there congruity between the research methodology and the interpretation of results?

(vi) Is there a statement locating the researcher culturally or theoretically?

(vii) Is the influence of the researcher on the research, and vice- versa, addressed?

(viii)   Are participants, and their voices, adequately represented?

(ix)   Is the research ethical according to current criteria or, for recent studies, and is there evidence of ethical approval by an appropriate body?, and

(x)   Do the conclusions-drawn in the research report flow from the analysis, or interpretation, of the data?

After searching, 2,407 articles were found. Using Endnote software, the titles and the abstracts of the articles were checked, and 905 duplicate articles were removed. Then the titles and the abstracts of 1,502 articles were examined by the researchers. A total of 1,350 irrelevant articles were excluded based on the study objectives. At this stage, in case of doubting the relevance of an article with the study objectives, the full text of the article was reviewed by the researchers. In the next step, a search was done to access the full texts of the articles and, finally, the full text of 152 articles were reviewed. Considering the inclusion and the exclusion criteria based on the research objectives, some articles were excluded for the reasons given in the Prisma flowchart. To ensure that all the articles had been retrieved, the reference lists of the final articles were also manually searched; no studies were added in this stage. Finally, 54 studies were finalized.

This systematic review study was conducted with the aim of explaining Individuals' near-death experiences and identifying common experiences. The results of this study are categorized into four main categories including emotional, cognitive, religious, spiritual and supernatural experiences.

## 3.2   Supernatural Experiences of NDErs

Supernatural experiences were the most frequent category of experiences related to NDE, which consist of two subcategories: out-of-body experiences (OBEs), and supernatural and metaphysical perceptions. In many studies, supernatural perceptions include passing through a tunnel involuntarily, moving toward the ceiling [out-of-body experience (OBE)], seeing one's own physical body from above whilst outside the body (the phenomenon of self-bilocation), having awareness of the places far from the body, self-permeability (passing through physical objects such as walls), being present in several locations at the same time (self-multilocation) (composed bodies), the feeling of being floating, entering a non-terrestrial location (heaven), and telepathy (non-verbal communication) with others.

It can be said that the most important feature of NDEs is an out-of-body experience (OBE), which had been experienced by the majority of the NDErs. OBE is a type of autoscopy (literally, "watching oneself") in which the soul is separated from the body, but the individual is in a fully conscious state or beyond normal consciousness. Soul, in religion and philosophy, the immaterial aspect or essence of a human being that which confers individuality and humanity, often considered to be synonymous with the mind or the self. For most theologies, the Soul is further defined as that part of the individual, which partakes of divinity and transcends the body in different explanations. The individual seems to be awake, and watches his body and the world from a disembodied place and outside his physical body, or perceives verified events that have occurred at a distance outside his/her scope. A typical narrative is: "I was lying on the bed. Suddenly, I ascended in a suspended state, watching myself and the events that were taking place from somewhere above the floor, for example, near the ceiling."

After an OBE, some individuals have had numerous supernatural perceptions. In some cases, there is a higher number of perceived experiences and, in others, there are fewer ones. However, there are many commonalities among the mentioned metaphysical experiences. The results of various studies show that after the soul leaves the body, NDErs enter a cylindrical tunnel, at the beginning of which there is absolute darkness and, at the end, a very dazzling light toward which the individual is guided. In most cases, this experience has been a very difficult one to forget. This experience is called a

Tunnel Experience. A tunnel experience may be defined as the perception of a realistic enclosed space which is much longer than its diameter. The peripheral features and the deep perspectives of this phenomenon indicate organizing the space around a central area in the visual field. Tunnel experiences have been reported in different forms including cylinder, pipe, tunnel, passage, corridor, spiral, well, funnel, shaft, hole, culvert, cave, long enclosure, sewer, cone, and so on. Crossing the tunnel occurs mostly for Indian and Buddhist NDEr's. However, the results of another study conducted on the Muslim population have also confirmed similar experiences. In a study, it was stated that tunnels are not seen or are very rare in Thai NDEs. This systematic review study shows that the supernatural and metaphysical experiences of the participants have similar roots for every race and religion, with differences in the expression of details.

## 3.3   Spiritual and Religious Experiences of NDErs

The second category of NDEs were spiritual and religious experiences, consisting of four subcategories: (i) meeting with the dead and acquaintances, (ii) meeting with religious figures, (iii) feeling of oneness with the universe, and (iv) observing punishment and reward for actions.

Some NDEr's have reported encounters with their deceased relatives and friends. Additionally, some children who have experienced NDEs have reported meeting the individuals whom they did not know at the time of the NDE, but later recognized as their deceased relatives from the family photos they had never seen before. Other NDErs report encountering a recently deceased individual, whose death they hadn't been aware of. One of the common aspects of the experiences was meeting with religious figures. The results of a study that compared NDE experiences in different cultures show that in western NDEs, when one is in the tunnel, he/she perceives that a group of deceased relatives and friends have come to welcome him/her, while in Thai NDEs, the experiences usually start with Yama toots (Yamdoots are the messengers of death according to Hinduism, the agents of Yama, the god of the netherworld). In Thai

NDEs, there is no experience of being light, and the Buddha appears only symbolically. One of the Thai experienced mentioned, "I asked [Yama toot] to take me to visit the Lord Buddha. I told him I had to see the Buddha. Yama toot looked up and pointed at the sky, saying, 'That big star is the Buddha'". In Western NDEs, the majority of the NDErs were Christians, and had seen the figures associated with Jesus Christ and the apostles. In a study whose target population were from the largest branch of Shia Islam comprising about 85 percent of all Shia Muslims, the reported religious and spiritual figures. For a better understanding of this category, the individuals' religious and cultural backgrounds should be considered while interpreting the experiences, encounters, and observations.

The results of some other studies reveal a feeling of oneness with the universe and the whole cosmos, where the NDErs had stated that they had unified with the whole universe or a part of creation such as plants, with no distance between them. The idea that the individual is inextricably connected to the rest of the world, or that everything is part of a whole, can be found in many of the world's religious, spiritual, and philosophical traditions. Most of the individuals who have experienced the feeling of oneness say that they will choose this state of mind if they have eternal life. Oneness is perhaps the deepest and the most sublime state that a human being can achieve. The last subcategory of spiritual-religious experiences was observing punishment and reward for actions. Research shows that some NDEr's are able to perceive the external consequences of their actions and deeds in the world, as well as their inner and hidden effects.

## 3.4   Cognitive Experiences of NDErs

Another category of NDEs were cognitive experiences, which consisted of four subcategories, including (i) heightened senses, (ii) an altered nature of time, (iii) reviewing life events, and (iv) the sudden perception of a specific knowledge.

In regard with the heightened senses, a review of the reports of the NDEr's shows that their visual descriptions are impressive (efficacious) and clear (obvious), all while these individuals are unconscious and often clinically dead at the time of experiencing and seeing such wonderful sights. In NDEs, all the senses of sight, hearing, touch, taste, and smell have been described. The heightened senses and the improved consciousness among these individuals even indicate that these experiences are to be very different from dreams and sleep, and at the moment it is difficult to find a recognized medical explanation for NDEs. This phenomenon is medically inexplicable. There is no other type of altered consciousness experience in which events are that clear, consciousness is that strong, and events follow one another in such a specific order. The research conducted in this field shows a stable pattern of enhanced consciousness and heightened senses, which leads to the clarity of NDEs and proves them. Moreover, according to some experienced, in NDEs, time loses its meaning and sense, and they see the events of their life in a fraction of a second.

## 3.5   Reviewing the Past Events by NDErs

Reviewing the past events of one's life is another cognitive experience in which NDErs may see a part or all of their life. The individual's encounter with self is one of the most important and common features of these experiences. At this stage, one encounters his/her own words, actions, and thoughts, and sees his/her own life in the form of a book, show, or movie, and judges it. The results of other research show that while reviewing their lives, the individuals review their past actions, words, and thoughts, and realize that each of them has a special significance, which has affected both themselves and others in this world. In addition, the results of various studies state that the events observed in the NDEr's life reviews are based on reality. These results assume that if NDEs are real, it is expected that the events observed during the life review be confirmed by the individual, and vice versa, if NDEs are not real, significant errors must occur during the life review. However, the latter is not the case, and everything has been confirmed by the individuals.

## 3.6    Emotional Experiences of NDErs

The last category of near-death experiences is emotional experiences, which includes two subcategories: (i) positive experiences and (ii) negative experiences.

Many NDErs state that they have experienced immense peace, and that it has been their most memorable experience, in such a way that they hesitated whether or not to return to life. In addition, in the cases where an individual had died with severe pain, his/her pain had disappeared with the sudden experience of relaxation. Most of the early studies on NDEs depicted only positive emotions. However, an interdisciplinary study was published, in which they identified 55 NDErs, eleven of whom reported negative experiences. Another study indicated that 1–10% of the samples had not described positive feelings, these different proportions can be attributed to very broad definitions of disturbing NDEs, as well as different methods. Reviewing the conducted studies shows that hellish and purgatory scenes are rarely found in NDEs, but heavenly scenes are seen more often and are very similar to each other. It may be concluded that the disturbing dimensions of the experience, added to its mystical aspect, can prevent the individuals from sharing it.

Based on the results of a study, frightening NDEs are divided into three groups:

(i)    The negative events may be viewed as warnings about unwise actions, leading to self-analysis and, ultimately, a "spin" in the NDEr's life,

(ii)    The NDEr may treat the event as if it is not important, and

(iii)    The frightening event may lead to difficulty in integrating the experience, developing a sense of stigma.

In this study conducted by Hashemi, et al. it shows a stable pattern of enhanced consciousness and heightened senses, "which leads to the clarity of NDEs and proves their being real." The familiarity of the treatment staff, especially nurses and doctors, with NDE components and elements, gaining knowledge in this regard, and an awareness of appropriate and pertinent interventions can lead to proper reactions and feedbacks in response to the NDErs.

## 3.7 Results of World's Largest Near-Death Experiences Study

Recollections in relation to death, so-called out-of-body experiences (OBEs) or near-death experiences (NDEs), are an often spoken about phenomenon which have frequently been considered hallucinatory or illusory in nature; however, objective studies on these experiences are limited.

In 2008, a large-scale study involving 2060 patients from 15 hospitals in the United Kingdom, United States and Austria was launched. The **AWARE** (**AWA**reness during **RE**suscitation) study examined the broad range of mental experiences in relation to death. Researchers also tested the validity of conscious experiences using objective markers for the first time in a large study to determine whether claims of awareness compatible with out-of-body experiences correspond with real or hallucinatory events.

Results of the study have been published in the journal Resuscitation and are now available online.

## 3.8 Conclusions of the Study

The study concludes:

- The themes relating to the experience of death appear far broader than what has been understood so far, or what has been described as so-called near-death experiences (NDEs).

- In some cases of cardiac arrest, memories of visual awareness compatible with so-called out-of-body experiences may correspond with actual events.

- A higher proportion of people may have vivid death experiences, but do not recall them due to the effects of brain injury or sedative drugs on memory circuits.

- Widely used yet scientifically imprecise terms such as near-death and out-of-body experiences may not be sufficient to describe the actual experience of death. Future studies should focus on cardiac arrest, which is biologically synonymous with death, rather than ill-defined medical states sometimes referred to as 'near-death'.

- The recalled experience surrounding death merits a genuine investigation without prejudice.

Dr. Sam Parnia, Assistant Professor of Critical Care Medicine and Director of Resuscitation Research at The State University of New York at Stony Brook, USA, and the study's lead author, explained: "Contrary to perception, death is not a specific moment but a potentially reversible process that occurs after any severe illness or accident causes the heart, lungs and brain to cease functioning. If attempts are made to reverse this process, it is referred to as 'cardiac arrest'; however, if these attempts do not succeed it is called 'death'. In this study we wanted to go beyond the emotionally charged yet poorly defined term of NDEs to explore objectively what happens when we die."

Thirty-nine per cent of patients who survived cardiac arrest and were able to undergo structured interviews described a perception of awareness, but interestingly did not have any explicit recall of events.

"This suggests more people may have mental activity initially but then lose their memories after recovery, either due to the effects of brain injury or sedative drugs on memory recall," explained Dr. Parnia, who was an Honorary Research Fellow at the University of Southampton when he started the AWARE study.

Among those who reported a perception of awareness and completed further interviews, 46 per cent experienced a broad range of mental recollections in relation to death that were not compatible with the commonly used term of NDE's. These included fearful and persecutory experiences. Only 9 per cent had experiences compatible with NDEs and 2 per cent exhibited full awareness compatible with OBEs with explicit recall of 'seeing' and 'hearing' events.

One case was validated and timed using auditory stimuli during cardiac arrest. Dr. Parnia concluded: "This is significant, since it has often been assumed that experiences in relation to death are likely hallucinations or illusions, occurring either before the heart stops or after the heart has been successfully restarted, but not an experience corresponding with 'real' events when the heart isn't beating. In this case, consciousness and awareness appeared to occur during a three-minute period when there was no heartbeat. This is paradoxical, since the brain typically ceases functioning within 20-30 seconds of the heart stopping and doesn't resume again until the heart has been restarted. Furthermore, the detailed recollections of visual awareness in this case were consistent with verified events.

"Thus, while it was not possible to absolutely prove the reality or meaning of patients' experiences and claims of awareness, (due to the very low incidence of around 2 per cent) the explicit recall of visual awareness or so-called OBEs, it was impossible to disclaim them either and more work is needed in this area. Clearly, the recalled experience surrounding death now merits further genuine investigation without prejudice."

## 3.9   Near-death Experiences: Fact or fantasy?

"Suddenly amidst all this pain I saw a light very faint and in the distance. It got nearer to me, and everything was so quiet; it was warm, I was warm, and all the pain began to go. I was finally there, and I felt as if someone had put his arms around me. I was safe, no more pain, nothing, just this lovely, caring sensation."

The above quote above comes from a 48-year-old woman who, on one occasion, almost died from complications related to a spinal tumor; it evokes much of the general emotion associated with a classic near-death experience story.

The term "near-death experience" (NDE) is well-known throughout America and many other countries. Most cultures have an equivalent experience; even children have related NDEs.

An NDE might involve walking toward a bright light at the end of a tunnel, meeting gods, speaking with relatives who are long-dead, out-of-body experiences (OBEs) or feeling bathed in light.

Almost unanimously, it is a significant life experience, conversations about NDEs are often accompanied by discussions of the afterlife and the mind surviving the mortal body.

These kinds of esoteric tales would normally be banished to the realms of pseudoscience and parapsychology, but their pervasive nature – an estimated 3 percent of Americans report having experienced an NDE – has sparked a smattering of genuine scientific research and a wealth of conjecture.

## 3.10   What do NDEs consist of?

One Dutch study, published in The Lancet, set out to investigate the regularity of NDEs and tried to tease apart causal factors.

The investigators reported that 50 percent of individuals who experienced an NDE mentioned an awareness of being dead, 56 percent regarded it a positive experience, 24 percent reported an OBE, 31 percent described traveling through a tunnel and 32 percent spoke of interacting with deceased people.

This study also showed that, of the patients interviewed, although all were clinically dead at one point, only a small percentage (18 percent) experienced, or remembered, the NDE. The likelihood of having an NDE was not related to the level of cerebral anoxia (lack of oxygen to the brain), the amount of preceding fear or the type of medication they were taking.

According to a paper, NDEs were more often experienced by patients under 60, and women more commonly described deeper experiences. Conversely, those with memory deficits following resuscitation were less likely to report NDEs, which is to be expected.

There is obviously something driving these experiences, but the factors that impact them are still very much up for debate.

## 3.11  Cultural Flexibility in NDEs

The NDE phenomenon is particularly fascinating because the psychological and physiological factors are intimately tied to social and cultural factors. For instance, the NDE of a 40-year-old white male from Nebraska might include visions of a shimmering white, bearded male beckoning him through pearl-encrusted gates; the NDE of a 12-year-old boy from Papa New Guinea probably will not. The Mapuche people of South America and residents of Hawaii are more likely to see landscapes and volcanoes, whereas NDEs in Thailand and India rarely involve landmarks, tunnels or light; for Tibetans, light features more heavily, as do illusions of reincarnation.

The following narrative comes from an African NDE, reported in 1992.

A young man had been attacked by a lioness after attempting to capture one of her cubs. He narrated the following:

"I could see myself going into some kind of a trance. A highway suddenly opened up before me. It seemed to be going endlessly into the sky. Along it were a lot of stars, also spreading up to the sky. Each time I tried to get on the highway, the stars would block my way. I just stood there not knowing what to do. After a while, the highway and stars disappeared. I woke up and found myself in a hospital bed."

Europeans and North Americans often visualize beautiful gardens; intriguingly, the Kalai of Melanesia are more inclined to see an industrialized world of factories.

Culture and a person's hopes or dreams clearly influence the nature of NDEs; but what biological mechanisms could be behind this strange phenomenon?

## 3.12   What is behind NDEs?

A phenomenon so widely experienced cannot be dismissed as just another old wives' tale; there has to be something biology at work to explain its prevalence.

Some observers claim that NDEs display a rift in current neuroscientific theory, and that the experience shows another, more esoteric facet to our existence. Many believe we should split the mind from the functions of the brain, once and for all.

However, this type of thinking is not necessary to explain NDEs; rather than claiming paranormal origins, the field of cognitive neuroscience has attacked the problem as it would any other: as an output of the brain.

There are a few potential explanations, any number of which might be involved in each individual's experience. The following are some attempts to explain the biological origin of NDEs.

Often, NDEs are reported as a euphoric, blissful experience. At first glance, this seems paradoxical, given the circumstances surrounding NDEs. However, a number of recreational drugs have been found to closely mimic the visual and emotional aspects of NDEs.

One such drug – ketamine – that is used both recreationally and as an anesthetic, can produce hallucinations, OBEs, euphoria, dissociation, and spiritual experiences. Ketamine produces these effects by acting at N-methyl-D-aspartate (NMDA) receptors, the same receptors utilized by other recreational drugs, such as amphetamines.

When an animal is under extreme stress, dopamine and opioid pathways are known to trigger. These reward pathways seem to come into play during traumatic events; although we do not know exactly why this should be, they no doubt evolved to be of assistance in times of extreme danger.

A brain in shock, being flooded by natural opioids, can go some of the way to explaining the intense feelings of quiet and calm.

## 3.13   The Tunnel of Light

Possibly the most well-known facet of an NDE is the feeling of being drawn into a long tunnel with a bright light at the end. Some researchers believe that this phenomenon can be explained by retinal ischemia (lack of oxygen to the retina).

The theory goes that, as the retina is starved of oxygen, peripheral vision slowly decays and only the centre of the visual field can be seen. Tunnel vision is a symptom of both extreme fear and oxygen loss (hypoxia), both of which are often present during the process of dying.

No doubt, NDEs are a complex phenomenon with a myriad of mechanisms behind them. From a lack of oxygen affecting the visual system to a brain struggling to make sense of strange emotions; from the drug-like triggering of reward pathways and a host of cultural expectations. Being close to death (or believing that you are) is a unique physiological and psychological experience. It is little wonder that it produces such a confusion of sights and sounds.

The precise nature of each NDE will not be unraveled for many years. After all, catching them in action, at one of the most critical points of an individual's life is no easy task, and the ethics of experimental interventions could prove tricky.

One thing is for sure, NDEs are fascinating, and a worthy topic of further research.

CHAPTER 4

# FURTHER STUDIES ON OUT-OF-BODY AND NEAR-DEATH EXPERIENCES

## 4.1  Out-of-Body and Near-Death Experiences

Out-of-Body experiences (OBEs) and Near-Death Experiences (NDEs) have accompanied and fascinated humanity since times immemorial and have long been the province of circles interested in the occult. Many authors have even argued that these experiences provide evidence for mind-brain independence or even the persistence of life after death. The neurology of OBEs and NDEs takes a different stance and proposes to study the brain mechanisms that are associated with these experiences. Accordingly, OBEs have been studied by neurologists and cognitive scientists, as they allow to investigate the functional and neural mechanisms of bodily awareness and self-consciousness in specific brain regions. In the present article we shall review these recent neuroscientific data on OBEs. The situation is quite different for NDEs. Although many different theories have been proposed about putative (generally considered) underlying brain processes, neurologists and cognitive neuroscientists have paid little attention to these experiences. This is unfortunate, because the scientific study of NDEs could provide insights into the functional and neural mechanisms of many facets of human experience such as beliefs, concepts, personality, spirituality, magical thinking, and the self. Moreover, as we shall see, there is a frequent confusion between OBEs and NDEs. This is probably due to the fact that OBEs are often associated with NDE, if not one of the NDE key feature. In the following, we will describe OBEs and NDEs, providing definitions, incidences, key phenomenological features, and reviewing some relevant psychological and neurocognitive mechanisms.

## 4.2 Out-of-Body Experiences (OBEs)

### 4.2.1 Definition of OBE

In an OBE, people seem to be awake and feel that their 'self', or centre of experience, is located outside of the physical body. They report seeing their body and the world from an elevated extracorporeal location. The subject's reported perceptions are organized in such a way as to be consistent with this elevated visuo-spatial perspective. The following example from Irwin, illustrates what individuals commonly experience during an OBE: "I was in bed and about to fall asleep when I had the distinct impression that I was at the ceiling level looking down at my body in the bed. I was very startled and frightened; immediately [afterwards] I felt that I was consciously back in the bed again." We have defined an OBE by the presence of the following three phenomenological features: (i) the feeling of being outside of one's physical body (disembodiment); (ii) the perceived location of the self at a distanced and elevated visuo-spatial perspective (perspective); and (iii) the experience of seeing one's own body (autoscopy) from this elevated perspective. In other proposed definitions of OBEs it suffices to experience disembodiment. For example, a researcher defined OBEs as 'experiences in which the sense of self or the centre of awareness is felt to be located outside of the physical body' and Irwin, as experiences in which 'the centre of consciousness appears to the experient to occupy temporarily a position which is spatially remote from his/her body'. Another researcher's definition requires disembodiment and a distanced visuo-spatial perspective: 'the feeling of a spatial separation of the observing self from the body'. OBEs therefore seem to constitute a challenge to the experienced spatial unity of self and body under normal conditions, that is, the feeling that there is a 'real me' that resides in my body and is both the subject and agent of my experiences. Probably for this reason, OBEs have attracted the attention of philosophers, psychologists, and neurologists alike, and many have conceptualized OBEs as an extreme example of deviant bodily self-consciousness arising from abnormal brain processes that code for the feeling of embodiment under normal conditions.

### 4.2.2 Incidence of OBEs

How common are OBEs in the general population? This question is still difficult to answer for the following reasons: (i) different investigators have asked quite different questions about the presence of an OBE; (ii) have used different methods (mail, phone or personal interviews); and (iii) most studies have been carried out in populations of college students, mostly from anglo-saxon psychology departments. Depending on the questions asked, how they are asked, who the samples include and how an OBE is defined, the results are very likely to differ. Accordingly, it is not surprising that questionnaire studies have estimated the OBE incidence in the general population as ranging from 8% to 34%. Also the two key features (autoscopy and distanced visuo-spatial perspective), as used in recent neurobiologically-motivated studies by some researchers were not considered as necessary OBE-features in most of these surveys. According to one researcher, incidences above 10% are very likely overestimates and we conservatively suggest that 5% of the general population have experienced an OBE. From a cross-cultural point of view OBEs seem to occur and be part of folklore in many parts of the world, although to-date very few studies have investigated this interesting issue.

### 4.2.3 Neurology of OBEs

Only few neurological cases with OBEs have been reported in the last 50 years. Subsequently, further cases were reported. OBEs have been observed predominantly in patients with epilepsy and migraine. Some researchers reported migraine patients with OBEs to be 11%.

The reviewed data point to an important involvement of the right TPJ (temporo-parietal junction) in OBEs of neurological origin. The observation that electrical stimulation of this area may induce OBEs and other abnormal own body perceptions further suggests that during OBEs the integration of proprioceptive, tactile, visual, and vestibular information of one's body fails, due to discrepant central own body representations. It has been suggested that autoscopic phenomena (including OBEs) result from a failure to integrate multisensory bodily information and proposed that they result from a disintegration in bodily or personal space (due to conflicting tactile, proprioceptive, kinesthetic, and visual signals) and a second disintegration between personal and extra-personal space (due to conflicting visual and vestibular signals caused by a vestibular otolithic dysfunction). While disintegration in personal space was present in all three forms of autoscopic phenomena, differences between the different forms of autoscopic phenomena were mainly due to differences in strength and type of the vestibular dysfunction. Following this model, OBEs were associated with a strong otolithic (related to a tiny, bonelike particle or stony, platelike structure in the internal ear of lower vertebrates) vestibular disturbance. This has recently been studied in healthy subjects, performed an evoked potential study and a transcranial magnetic stimulation study with healthy participants as well as intracranial electrode recordings in a patient with OBEs due to epilepsy. The evoked potential study showed the selective activation of the TPJ at 330–400 ms after stimulus onset when healthy volunteers imagined themselves in the position and visual perspective that is generally reported by people experiencing spontaneous OBEs. The transcranial magnetic stimulation study showed that magnetic interference with the TPJ during this same time period impaired performance in this task, as opposed to stimulation over a control site at the intraparietal sulcus. No such interference was observed for imagined spatial transformations of external objects, suggesting the selective implication of the TPJ in mental imagery of one's own body and OBEs. Moreover, in an epileptic patient with OBEs due to seizure activity at the TPJ, performing the own body imagery task, while evoked potentials were recorded from intracranial electrodes, the task-specific activation at the TPJ was found. These results suggest that the TPJ is a crucial structure for the conscious experience of the spatial unity of self and body, and that the researchers associated that the brain processing is disturbed in OBEs. We now turn to NDEs, which as we will see offer more insights into the mechanisms involved in OBEs.

## 4.3 Near-Death Experiences (NDEs)

In different life-threatening situations, people can sometimes experience vivid illusions and hallucinations as well as strong mystical and emotional feelings often grouped under the term of near-death experiences (NDEs). These medical situations seem to involve cardiac arrest, perioperative or post-partum complications, septic or anaphylactic shock, electrocution, coma resulting from traumatic brain damage, intracerebral hemorrhage or cerebral infarction, hypoglycemia, asphyxia, and apnea. To this date, systematic studies on the incidence of NDEs in verified medical conditions only exist for cardiac arrest patients. Other situations that are merely experienced as life-threatening have also been reported to be associated with NDEs, although they often are not objectively life-threatening (mild or not life-endangering diseases, depression, minor accidents, falls, and other circumstances).

### 4.3.1 Definitions of NDE

Several definitions have been attempted for NDEs. Moody, who coined the term NDE, defined it as 'any conscious perceptual experience which takes place during an event in which a person could very easily die or be killed but nonetheless survives'. Irwin defined NDEs as 'a transcendental experience precipitated by a confrontation with death' and Nelson et al. state that ' NDEs are responses to life-threatening crises characterized by a combination of dissociation from the physical body, euphoria, and transcendental or mystical elements.' Greyson proposed that NDEs are 'profound subjective experiences with transcendental or mystical elements, in which persons close to death may believe they have left their physical bodies and transcended the boundaries of the ego and the confines of space and time'. Many more such broad definitions of the NDE have been given rendering their scientific study difficult. They seem to include a large variety of phenomena and not all researchers may agree that the investigated phenomenon (or assembly of phenomena) of a given study, may actually concern NDEs or typical NDEs. Here-below, we have reviewed the most frequent and characteristic perceptual and cognitive features of NDEs. To complicate matters NDEs (just like OBEs) are difficult to study as their occurrence is generally unpredictable and they are usually not reported at their moment of occurrence, but days, months or even years later.

### 4.3.2   Incidence of NDEs

Early studies of NDEs among survivors of cardiac arrest, traumatic accidents, suicide attempts, and other life-threatening situations estimated an incidence of 48% by one researcher or 42% by another researcher. Greyson suggested that this rate is probably too high as these studies were retrospective, often carried out many years after the NDEs occurred, they were using self-selected populations, and lacked appropriate control populations. He rather estimated the incidence of NDEs between 9% and 18%. More recent and better controlled prospective studies focused on cardiac arrest patients and confirmed lower estimations, with values ranging between 6% and 12%. Some researchers found an incidence of 6.3%, Greyson of 10%, and other researchers of 12%. Yet, as is the case for OBEs, in the absence of a clear and widely accepted definition of NDEs, it will remain difficult to define the exact incidence of NDEs. In order to avoid this problem most recent studies have used a score above a certain value on Greyson's scale. Early studies failed to find demographic correlates of the NDE. Neither age, nor gender, race, occupational status, marital status or religiosity seemed to predict the probability to experience an NDE. More recently, a couple of researchers found that young age is associated with a higher probability of NDEs in cardiac arrest patients, although this finding might be confounded by increased medical recovery rates in younger cardiac arrest patients. Another finding is that women tend to have more intense NDEs than men, an observation that might partly be related to Moody's suggestion that women might be less afraid to report NDEs or the fact that women have been found to score generally higher on anomalous-perception questionnaires than male subjects. It is possible that having had an NDE facilitates the reoccurrence of such experiences, as 10% of subjects reported multiple NDEs. NDEs have been described in many different cultures and times. Although some consistency can be found in cross-cultural reports, the specific phenomenology (i.e., the structure and the contents of the experience) may nevertheless vary.

### 4.3.3 Phenomenology of NDEs

Moody initially listed 15 key features in NDEs. Yet, not one single NDE in his study included all 15 NDE features. Moreover, none of these 15 NDE features was present in all reported NDEs, and no invariable temporal sequence of features could be established. Due to these difficulties, standardized questionnaires have subsequently been developed to identify and measure more precisely the occurrence of NDEs and their intensity (or depth). Ring developed the 'Weighted Core Experience Index' on the basis of structured interviews of 102 persons who found themselves "near-death". The scale is based on 10 features that he gathered from the literature as well as interviews with people with NDEs. His 10 features were: (i) the subjective feeling of being dead, (ii) feelings of peace, (iii) bodily separation, (iv) entering a dark region, (v) encountering a presence or hearing a voice, (vi) experiencing a life review, (vii) seeing or being enveloped in light, (viii) seeing beautiful colours, (ix) entering into the light, and (x) encountering visible spirits. According to the presence or absence of each of these features, the score ranges between 0 and 29. This scale has been criticized because it is largely based on arbitrarily selected and weighted features, and seemed to contain several uncommon features of NDEs as estimated by other authors. Ring also elaborated a sequence of 5 NDE-stages, the presence of which he considered to be representative of the 'core NDE'. To address the aforementioned limitations, Greyson developed an NDE scale that has been used by many recent investigators. He began by selecting 80 features from the existing literature on NDEs and subsequently reduced these to 33 features. He further arrived at a final 16-item scale with a maximum score of 32. This questionnaire has been shown to have several advantages as compared to other questionnaires, especially good test-retest reliability and item score consistency. In his original study, Greyson defined four components of a NDE – cognitive, affective, paranormal, and transcendental – which he later reduced to a classification of three main types of NDEs, according to the specific dominance of the phenomenological components: (i) cognitive, (ii) affective, and (iii) transcendental types. In the following we describe the main phenomena that characterize NDEs.

### 4.3.4   OBEs in NDEs

OBE are considered a key feature of NDEs, although their frequency was found to vary greatly between different studies. Ring found that 37% of subjects with a NDE experienced disembodiment ('being detached from their body') of whom about half also experienced autoscopy. Greyson and Stevenson found an incidence of 75% of disembodiment (without detailing the presence of autoscopy or elevated visuo-spatial perspective). Sabom reported a 'sense of bodily separation' in 99%, a number in stark contrast with the figure of 24% found by other researchers. Disembodiment during NDEs has been reported to be accompanied by auditory and somatosensory sensations. NDE subjects with OBEs characterized by disembodiment and elevated visuo-spatial perspective often report seeing the scene of the accident or operating room. Greyson mentions the example of an NDE in a 26-year-old patient with pulmonary embolism: 'I (the real me, the soul, the spirit, or whatever) drifted out of the body and hovered near the ceiling. I viewed the activity in the room from this vantage point. The hospital room was to my right and below me. It confused me that the doctors and nurses in the room were so concerned about the body they had lifted to the bed. I looked at my body and it meant nothing to me. I tried to tell them I was not in the body'.

Future studies on OBEs during NDEs should characterize OBEs with respect to recently defined phenomenological characteristics and enquire systematically about the associated sensations as done in neurological patients (such as visual, auditory, bodily, or vestibular sensations) as well as the presence of disembodiment, autoscopy, elevated perspective permitting to distinguish between autoscopic hallucination, heautoscopy (a term used in psychiatry and neurology for the reduplicative hallucination of "seeing one's own body at a distance), and OBE. This will allow describing the phenomenology of OBEs during NDEs in more detail and allow relating these data to recent neurological and neurobiological observations on OBEs. Not much is currently known about whether OBEs that are associated with NDEs differ from OBEs without NDE features or whether NDEs, with or without OBEs differ. Alvarado found that OBEs in subjects who believed to be close to death were phenomenologically richer than those who did not, with more feelings of passing through a tunnel, hearing unusual sounds, and seeing spiritual entities. Two additional features reached statistical significance, namely seeing one's physical body and seeing lights. Of course, it might be the case that due to the very presence of these features these subjects believed they had been close to death. Owens et al. compared the phenomenology of NDEs in subjects being medically close to death with NDEs where subjects only believed to be close to death. They found that the former patients tended to report more often seen lights and enhanced cognition than the latter group. There were no significant differences between both groups in seeing a tunnel, having an OBE and a life review. Nelson et al. found that 76% of subjects with NDEs also experienced an OBE. 40% of these patients had their OBEs only as part of the NDE episode, 33% also had OBEs in other circumstances, and 26% had an OBE only in other circumstances, that is, not associated with the NDE. This last number was significantly higher than non-NDE-related OBEs in an age-matched control group of healthy subjects. Further links might exist between rare, so-called supernaturalistic OBEs, and OBEs during NDEs. Collectively, these data suggest that OBEs and NDEs may share some functional and brain mechanisms, but also point towards the involvement of distinct mechanisms.

### 4.3.5　The Tunnel and the Bright Light

Experiencing a passage through some darkness or a tunnel was experienced by 25% of subjects with NDEs. This may be associated with the sensation of movement of one's own body such as forward vection (a visual illusion of self-motion in a stationary observer), flying or falling, at varying speeds. Some researchers suggest that the experience of a tunnel is associated with the presence of severe medical conditions (such as cardiac arrest, drowning, trauma, profuse blood loss), as opposed to mild injuries, fear, or fatigue. In the following example: 'After I had floated close to the ceiling for a short time, I was sucked into a tunnel. It was black and dark around me, somewhat frightening, but this did not last long: at the end of the tunnel I saw a clear light towards which I travelled'. The tunnel experience or darkness may thus be associated with the subsequent experience of an intense light. It was found to be the case in half of the subjects with NDEs who reported the experience of a tunnel. Ring and Sabom found that 30% and other researchers found that 23% of subjects with NDE reported seeing a light, but did not specify if this was associated with the experience of a tunnel. The light is usually white or yellow, very bright, but not experienced as painful. It seems to cover a larger area in the visual field when subjects experience vection.

### 4.3.6 The Life Review

The life review has been defined as the perception of 'unusually vivid, almost instantaneous visual images of either the person's whole life or a few selected highlights of it. One person reports the following life review during a mountain fall: 'I saw my whole past-life take places in many images, as though on a stage at some distance from me. I saw myself as the chief character in the performance. Everything was transfigured as though by a heavenly light and everything was beautiful without grief, without anxiety, and without pain.' Life reviews were found in 13–30% of subjects with NDEs. Couple of researchers analyzed 122 subjects with NDEs and reported that the number of distinct life memories may range from a few images (one or two) to the impression of a rapid flow of countless images depicting their entire life. Some subjects reported that the life review unfolds with an infinite number of images, simultaneously ('all at once'). It is usually experienced very vividly, associated with bright colours and can occur as moving in chronological order or in the opposite order (i.e., ending or starting with childhood). It can also purportedly involve elements of the future. Two studies speculated that life reviews are especially frequent in drowning victims, as compared to other situations. Conversely, it seems that suicide survivors and children with NDEs rarely report life reviews.

### 4.3.7 Meeting of Spirits

People often report seeing or feeling different entities or people during NDEs. Greyson gives the following example from the report of a man admitted to the hospital due to cardiac disease: 'he experienced an apparent encounter with his deceased mother and brother-in-law, who communicated to him, without speaking, that he should return to his body'. The encounters are sometimes identified as supreme beings, pure energy, spiritual guides, angels, helpers, or familiar people, but also as demons or tormentors. These encounters are reported frequently during NDEs (40% of the subjects in Ring's study; 52% in Greyson's study: 'sense of deceased/religious spirits. Sometimes subjects report to feel (rather than see) the presence of an unfamiliar person, a mystical, or a supreme entity (reported by 26% of NDE subjects in Greyson.

The seen or felt person may also be familiar, but is most often a deceased relative or friend. Ring and Kelly found that 8% of seen or felt persons were dead relatives, whereas Fenwick (39%) and Van Lommel et al, (32%) found this more frequently. Kelly analyzed this feature further by comparing 74 people with NDEs who reported to have perceived one or more deceased relatives with 200 people with NDE who did not. She found that deceased relatives are more frequently reported than deceased friends or children (in this study only 4% of people with NDEs reported seeing persons that were alive at the time of the NDE. Encounters of dead relatives have long been reported in the occult literature as 'apparitions' and are supposed to be frequent in so-called 'deathbed vision'. Sometimes verbal or thought communication (often described as 'telepathic') has been reported to take place between the subject and the encounters. Physical interactions such as touch or embraces are sometimes described as well. Some of these features have also been reported in neurological patients with heautoscopy.

### 4.3.8 Positive and Negative Emotions

NDE reports often consist of feelings of peace and calm (and sometimes ecstasy), despite the experienced severity of the situation.

Whereas Ring found that 60% of subjects with a NDE reported feelings of peace (56%), Sabom noted such feelings in all of his subjects with NDE. Greyson analyzed the feelings of peace and joy separately and found 85% for peace and 67% for joy. A related feature might be the loss of pain sensations as subjects with NDE often report to be relieved from the unbearable pain they were enduring minutes earlier. Heim reports his own experience when falling from a cliff: 'There was no anxiety, no trace of despair, nor pain; but rather calm seriousness, profound acceptance, and a dominant mental quickness and sense of surety'. Many subjects also report feelings of absolute love, all-encompassing acceptation, often by a supreme entity which is associated with a radiant light. Nevertheless, NDEs may also be associated with negative emotions, ' hell '-like features, encounters with tormentors or frightfully devoid of any meaning. The exact incidence of such negative NDEs is not known, but is assumed to be rather low.

### 4.3.9   Other Features

In this section we have listed other NDE features about which less is known concerning their phenomenology, frequency, and association with other features. These features are realness, mental clarity, sense of time, mystical features, and the experience of border and return.

### 4.3.9.1   Realness and mental clarity:

Although NDEs are often described as highly realistic sensations, we were not able to find detailed estimates. In the literature we found reports that NDEs are often experienced as 'real ' or 'realer than real'. Some authors have argued that NDEs are qualitatively different from dreams or drug-induced hallucinations. As one subject wrote: 'For many years, it was the most real thing that ever happened to me. Yes, far more real and vivid than any real-life incident. It was so real, detailed and so vivid and consistent; in fact, so totally un-dreamlike'. Thus, many subjects with NDEs believe them to involve actual disembodiment, meeting of spirits, seeing of lights, or being in the afterworld rather than mere experiences thereof. These subjects are often reluctant to refer to NDEs in psychological or neurophysiological terms. Realness is sometimes also reported as mental clarity or cognitive enhancement. Owens et al. found that the report of clear experience, perception, and cognition was more frequent in subjects who suffered serious life-threatening conditions than those who only thought themselves in great biological danger. Greyson found that 44% of NDE subjects reported accelerated thought with their NDE. Heim also refers to this aspect during his mountain fall: 'All my thoughts and ideas were coherent and very clear, and in no way susceptible, as are dreams, to obliteration. The relationship of events and their probable outcomes were viewed with objective clarity, no confusion entered at all '.

### 4.3.9.2   Sense of time:

A distorted sense of time is a frequent feature of NDEs, but has not been described in detail in statistical and phenomenological terms. Heim reported that 'time became greatly expanded' during his fall. Greyson found that 67% of NDE subjects reported an alteration of the sense of time, whereas this was much less frequent in a control group of subjects without NDEs (4%). Based on the reviewed phenomenology we suggest that the presence of a distorted sense of time, mental clarity, and life review might co-occur in subjects with NDEs.

### 4.3.10   Mystical and Transcendental Features

A feeling of 'oneness ' with the universe or of 'cosmic unity' was present in 52% of subjects with NDEs in Greyson's study. Twenty per cent of Ring's subjects and 54% of Sabom's subjects with NDEs reported the 'visit' of a supernaturalistic environment. This value is considerably smaller in people reporting OBEs (1%), but more frequent in subjects who report multiple OBEs. Descriptions here vary considerably, but most often seem to involve the experience of seeing pleasant sights like cities of light, green and flowered meadows, and vivid colours. Sometimes, images reminiscent of religious iconography are perceived.

### 4.3.11 Border and Return

A symbolic or concretely perceived limit or border is sometimes reported by subjects with NDEs. Greyson found this in 41% and Van Lommel et al, in 8%. NDEs (and OBEs) are often reported to end abruptly without the experience of intentional control. A patient, resuscitated by electrical defibrillation after an anterior myocardial infarction, reported: 'It appeared to me that I had a choice to re-enter my body and take the chances of them [the medical staff] bringing me around or I could just go ahead and die, if I wasn't already dead. I knew I was going to be perfectly safe, whether my body died or not. They thumped me a second time. I re-entered my body just like that'. The immediate aftermath is frequently the return of pain and the realization that one is alive (similar observations have also been reported in neurological patients with OBEs and related experiences such as heautoscopy.

### 4.3.12 Folk-Psychological Accounts and Psychological Aspects

Following psychoanalytic theory, several researchers consider NDEs as a defence mechanism unfolding in a hopeless, life-threatening situation. A couple of researchers were influential with their suggestion that the experience during a NDE may reflect a form of depersonalization, whereby the endangered subject 'separates ' from the body and the current events in order to be 'dissociated ' from the unsupportable consequences of death and pain. A researcher was perhaps the first to propose a psychoanalytic theory of NDEs. Following Heim's accounts of NDEs in fall survivors, he suggested that 'persons faced with potentially inescapable danger attempt to exclude this unpleasant reality from consciousness and "replace" it with pleasurable fantasies which protect them from being paralyzed by emotional shock'. By this process, it was then argued that subjects 'split' into an observing self and a body. The OBE component of many NDEs, in particular, has been seen as the prototypic experiential correlate of this detachment. However, this psychoanalytic account has been criticized on several grounds, mostly because of the lack of empirical evidence for it and the differences between the symptoms of dissociation in psychiatric populations and the reports of NDE subjects, as well as many methodological and scientific concerns about psychoanalysis itself. Other psychological authors suggested that NDEs are the consequence of a human tendency to deny death, the release of archetypical concepts of death, or the (symbolic or literal) regression to the experience of coming to life. These approaches of NDEs suffer from the same methodological and scientific concerns as psychoanalytical propositions. More quantitative approaches have proposed to analyze psychological variables of people with NDEs, as estimated by interviews and questionnaire surveys. Yet, as with OBEs, no clear psychopathological features have been found and subjects with NDEs and without NDEs do not differ with respect to measures of intelligence, extraversion, neuroticism, or anxiety. Unfortunately, only a small number of subjects with NDEs have been studied in this systematic manner. People with NDEs were also found to report more often so-called paranormal experiences prior to their NDE, as well as other complex experiences such as OBEs, feelings of being united with the universe, feeling the presence of God and otherworldly entities, or having past-life memories. Kohr found similar tendencies in people with NDEs: they reported repeated OBEs and higher interest in dreams, past-lives, and meditation. This suggests that subjects with NDEs might differ from other subjects in being more open to unusual experiences (and also willing to report these) and being attentive to the so-called inner-states. People with NDEs as well as people with OBEs also score higher than control subjects on absorption (a measure that refers to the tendency to immerse in imagination and internal states) and the related trait of fantasy proneness (a tendency to have vivid hallucinations, blurred distinction between reality and imagination, enhanced sensory experiences and heightened visual imagery). also found significantly higher scores in their group of NDE subjects Neurology of NDEs Although several authors have speculated on the neurology of NDEs, there is an almost complete absence of neurological data. Medical and neurological conditions that have been associated with NDEs and that are associated with brain interference or brain damage are cardiac arrest, general anesthesia, temporal lobe epilepsy, electrical brain stimulation, and sleep abnormalities (e.g., REM intrusions).

## 4.4   Brain Anoxia in Cardiac Arrest Patients

The data reported in the large prospective describes several clinical characteristics of patients that are likely to report a NDE after cardiac arrest. In most of these patients, cardiac arrest occurred in the hospital (in 234; 68%) and resuscitation was initiated within 2 minutes after cardiac arrest (in 190; 81%). Loss of consciousness lasted less than 5 minutes (in 187; 80%). Yet, loss of consciousness was diagnosed independently of a neurological or electroencephalographic examination and estimated only by electrocardiogram records resuscitation. A researcher defined 'clinical death (independent of neurological data) as a period of unconsciousness caused have shown that diffusion-weighted MRI may allow to reveal correlates of cerebral anoxia in cardiac arrest patients independent of severity of anoxia, that is, even in patients who recover very well. Moreover, standard MRI may not always reveal brain damage in these patients. It thus seems that different techniques of MRI in the acute as well as the chronic phase in such patients will be necessary to reveal potential functional and structural lesions causing distinct features of NDEs. Several authors have argued that brain anoxia may account for the auditory, visual, and memory aspects of NDEs (heard noises, perceived lights and tunnels, life review, encounters). Experiential phenomena have also been induced by electrical cortical stimulation of the temporal lobe, the hippocampus, and the amygdala, as well as the frontal and the parietal cortex.

## 4.5   Sleep Abnormalities and Brainstem Mechanisms

Recently it has been suggested that subjects with NDEs report more frequently symptoms that might be associated with a sleep disorder associated with REM intrusions (or rapid eye movement intrusions) as compared to age-matched control subjects without NDEs. This was especially the case in subjects who had NDEs with OBEs (whether as part of their NDE or occurring at a different time. REM intrusions were estimated based on questions such as 'Just before falling asleep or just after awakening, have you ever seen things, objects or people that others cannot see? ' and ' Have you ever awakened and found that you were unable to move or felt paralyzed? '. Both items were reported significantly more often in subjects with NDEs. Visual and auditory hallucinations were also reported to be more frequent in subjects with OBEs during NDEs It has been suggested that NDEs and OBEs may be related to muscular atonia during REM intrusions due to abnormal brainstem processing. REM intrusions are relatively frequent in the normal population and associated with sleep paralysis (a temporary paralysis of the body during sleep–wake transitions) in about 6% of the population. Symptoms similar to NDEs are also found in other medical conditions involving sleep or brainstem disturbances such as narcolepsy (a disorder involving excessive daytime sleepiness, peduncular hallucinations, hypnagogic and hypnopompic hallucinations, as well as sleep paralysis. Finally, patients with Guillain-Barré syndrome (an acute autoimmune disturbance of the peripheral nervous system leading in some cases to severe peripheral sensorimotor deficits that may require intensive care) have also been reported to have OBEs as well as NDE-like features. In a series of 139 such patients, mental disturbances have been found in 31% and included vivid and unusual dreams, visual illusions and hallucinations, as well as paranoid delusions. Interestingly, REM sleep was highly abnormal in these particular patients. The investigators did not inquire about OBEs directly, but some patients reported relevant phenomena such as vivid or dreamlike sensations of losing the sense of one's body, meeting people, hovering or floating weightlessly over their body, or having the impression to have left one's body. Moreover, patients with the Guillain-Barré syndrome also reported complex own body illusions that have been linked functionally to OBEs such as illusory body-part dislocations, the inversion-illusion, and room-tilt illusion.

## 4.6   Cognitive Neuroscience of NDE Phenomena

The reviewed data suggest that many functional and neural mechanisms are involved in the generation of the wide range of phenomena grouped under the term NDE. These mechanisms include mainly visual, vestibular, multisensory, memory, and motor mechanisms. Concerning brain regions the reviewed studies suggest damage to and/or interference with different cortical, subcortical, and brainstem mechanisms, as well as the peripheral nervous system. Interference with the functioning of this extended network also seems to occur in situations characterized by stress, physical exhaustion, rapid accelerations or decelerations, and deliberate relaxation. Although the neural mechanisms of many illusions and hallucinations have been described in detail, there are – at this stage – not even preliminary data on the neurology of the different phenomena associated with NDEs. Systematic neurological research is needed to fill this gap as has already been done for related experiences (such as the OBE) or related medical conditions in cardiac arrest patients (coma, vegetative state, minimally conscious states). Although abnormalities in brainstem and peripheral nervous system may lead to NDE phenomena, it is argued that major insights into these experiences will be gained by applying research techniques from cognitive neurology and cognitive neuroscience to NDE phenomena in order to reveal their cortical and subcortical mechanisms. Some NDE phenomena can be linked to distinct brain mechanisms. This was shown for the OBE (damage to right TPJ), tunnel vision and seeing of foveal lights (bilateral occipital damage including the optic radiation with macular sparing and/or foveal hallucinations), feeling of a presence and meeting of spirits (damage to left TPJ), as well as memory flashbacks, life review, and enhanced emotions (hippocampal and amygdala damage). All structures have been shown to be frequently damaged in those cardiac arrest patients that show excellent recovery and who are so far the best studied patient group with NDE phenomena.

SECTION-II:

# NEAR-DEATH-EXPERIENCE: SOME TRUE STORIES

# CHAPTER 5

# NEAR-DEATH EXPERIENCE OF ANITA MOORJANI

Anita Moorjani (born 16 March 1959) is the author of five books, including the New York Times bestseller, "Dying to be Me".

After she was diagnosed with stage-1-A Hodgkin's lymphoma in 2002, and rejected conventional treatment, Moorjani was taken to a hospital in 2006 where she lay in a coma for 30 hours, during which Moorjani claims to have undergone a **Near-Death Experience (NDE)**.

## 5.1   Early Life and Education of Anita Moorjani

Moorjani was born to Sindhi Indian parents Hargobind (father) and Neelu (mother) Shamdasani in Singapore. Shortly after her birth, her family moved to Sri Lanka, and when she was two years old, the family moved to Hong Kong, where she and her older brother Anoop grew up. Moorjani and her brother both studied in British schools. As an ethnic minority in a majority British school, Moorjani says she was often the victim of bullying. Moorjani's parents are Indian, and because of her diverse cultural background, she grew up as multilingual, speaking Sindhi, Cantonese, and English simultaneously.

Anita currently lives in Hong Kong with her husband, Danny, and when she is not traveling and speaking at conferences, she works as an intercultural consultant for multinational corporations based in the city.

## 5.2  Near-Death Experience (NDE) of Anita Moorjani

In February 2002, while living and working in Hong Kong, Moorjani was diagnosed with lymphoma after finding a lump on her neck. Initially, Moorjani rejected conventional medicine. She had watched several people close to her who had died of cancer, including her brother-in-law and her best friend, despite extensive conventional treatments. Over the months that ensued, Moorjani experimented with various alternative healing practices but to no avail. She subsequently underwent several conventional cancer treatments. However, by that point, despite beginning these treatments as she was brought into hospital, her doctors informed her and her family that it was "too late" to save her life. The lymphoma had spread throughout her body and had metastasized. At that point, all of Moorjani's organs had shut down, and she entered into a coma.

Moorjani came out of the coma 30 hours later. During those 30 hours, Moorjani asserts that she experienced many characteristic details of a near-death experience. Her account includes an **out-of-body experience (OBE)** with observations and awareness of physical surroundings. Moorjani said she had a strong reluctance to return to her suffering and dying physical body but was encouraged to return by her father and her best friend who told her that she needed to return and to "live her life fearlessly."

Subsequent to coming out of her coma, Moorjani's tumors shrank by about 70% within four days, and within five weeks she was cancer-free and released from the hospital, although she had to spend a few months in physiotherapy to regain her strength and the use of all her muscles and limbs. Moorjani remains cancer-free to this day.

## 5.3  Professional life of Anita Moorjani

Moorjani submitted the description of her NDE and subsequent healing to the Near-Death Experience Research Foundation (NDERF) website, a site owned and run by oncologist Jeffrey Long and his wife, Jody Long, a family law attorney.

Moorjani's story came to the attention of American self-help author, Wayne Dyer, who contacted his publishers, Hay House, asking them to locate her and suggest that she write a book, which they would publish.

**"Dying to be Me"** was published in March 2012, and hit The New York Times bestsellers list two weeks after its release. Moorjani was then invited to be on Wayne Dyer's PBS special titled "Wishes Fulfilled", and since then, she has been interviewed on "Fox and Friends," CNN's "Anderson Cooper 360," National Geographic International, Karen Davila's "HeadStart" on ANC Philippines, and many others. "Dying to be Me" has subsequently sold over a million copies worldwide, and has been published in more than 40 languages.

In January 2016, Moorjani's case attracted the attention of Dr. Oz, who scrutinized her medical records, and subsequently invited her to be on his show.

In the years following, Moorjani has published three additional books: "What if this is Heaven" (Hay House 2016), a self-published children's book "Love - A Story About Who You Truly Are" (2017), and most recently, the self-empowering "Sensitive is the New Strong" (Simon and Schuster, 2021).

## 5.4   Medical Explanation of Recovery from Cancer

Oncologist hematologist T.K. Chan, who treated Moorjani at the critical stage of her illness, ascribed her recovery to the draining of her lungs carried out by medical specialists after she was admitted to hospital, followed by chemotherapy which she had refused for four years. Chan stated "with lymphoma, it's never too late" and "Hodgkin's disease is quite curable; it can have a dramatic response to chemotherapy".

## 5.5   Details of Anita's Journey to Death

Anita developed serious problems in her body due to an advanced stage of cancer. As she was being rushed to the hospital, the world around her started to appear surreal and dreamlike, and she could feel herself slip further and further away from consciousness. She arrived at the hospital in a coma, only to find that the doctors were bleak—if not hopeless—in their evaluation of her chances. This wasn't the same place where she would usually visit for her treatments throughout the duration of her illness. The facility she had been going to over the years was more like a large clinic than a full-blown hospital. It had been adequate for what her doctor prescribed in the past, but it wasn't equipped to deal with medical emergencies. It was her choice all along to be treated at the smaller neighborhood institution because it was less intimidating—and she absolutely hated hospitals. She feared them because of the two people she had lost. Her best friend and Danny's (Anita's husband's) brother-in-law both died in large, cancer-specialist hospitals.

But when Danny called the clinic the morning she fell into a coma, her doctor told him to rush her to one of the largest and best-equipped hospitals in Hong Kong, where the doctor would have a team of specialists waiting for her. So this was the first time she was in this particular place and the first time she was being treated by this particular medical team.

The moment the oncologist saw her, her face visibly filled with shock. "Your wife's heart may still be beating," she told Danny, but she's not really in there. It's too late to save her."

Who's the doctor talking about? Anita wondered. She had never felt better in her life! "And why do Mum and Danny look so frightened and worried? Mum, please don't cry. What's wrong? Are you crying because of me? Don't cry! I'm fine—really, dear Mama, I am!" Anita thought she was speaking these words aloud, but nothing came out. She had no voice.

Anita wanted to hug her mother, comfort her and tell her that she was fine; and she couldn't comprehend why she (Anita) was unable to do so. Why was her physical body not cooperating? Why was she just lying there, limp, when all she wanted to do was to hug her beloved husband and mother, assuring them that she was fine and no longer in pain?

Because of the gravity of the situation, the doctor immediately called for another senior oncologist to back her up. In this near-death state, Anita was more acutely aware of all that was going on around her than she had ever been in a normal physical state. She wasn't using her five biological senses, yet she was keenly taking everything in, much more so than if she had been using her physical organs. It was as though another, completely different type of perception kicked in, and more than just perceive, she seemed to also encompass everything that was happening, as though she was slowly merging with it all.

The senior oncologist immediately ordered a medical team to wheel Anita's gurney (a wheeled stretcher used for transporting hospital patients) to the radiology lab so that they could do a full-body scan. Anita noticed that her head was still propped up at an angle with pillows, just as it had been at home the last few days. This was because her lungs were so filled with fluid that if her head lay flat, she would choke on her own fluids.

Anita was still connected to the portable oxygen tank, and when she reached the radiology lab, they removed the mask from her face, lifted her up, and put her in the MRI machine. Within a few seconds, she started choking, coughing, and sputtering.

"Please don't remove the oxygen—and she can't lie down flat! Please, she's choking! She can't breathe! She's going to die if you do this!" she heard Danny, her husband, cry out to the medical team.

"We really need to do this," explained one of the radiologists. "Please don't worry. We'll be as gentle as we can. She can handle about 30 seconds off the oxygen at a time."

So the radiologist slid Anita out of the MRI capsule every 30 or 40 seconds to put the oxygen mask over her face, then removed it and slid her back in again. As a result, the scan took a very long time to complete. After they finished, they wheeled her to the intensive care unit (ICU).

The medical team took what action they could, spurred on by Anita's husband's insistence that they not give up on me. While the minutes ticked by, she lay in the ICU as the staff administered treatments by way of needles and tubes, and her helpless family looked on.

A thick curtain was then drawn all around Anita's bed, separating her from the patients on either side of her. Danny and her mother were both on the outside of the cubicle created by the curtain. Anita noticed that the nurses were still scurrying (hurrying) around, preparing to hook up her near-lifeless body to the hospital's oxygen and other machinery to start an intravenous flow of fluids and glucose, since she was seriously malnourished. There was a monitor above her bed, and they started connecting her so that they could measure her blood pressure and heart rate. A food tube was inserted through her nose, down the back of her throat, and into her stomach so that she could be fed directly, and oxygen was being pumped through her nose via a respirator. They had trouble inserting the food tube and sliding it down her trachea (the tube in the throat that carries air to the lungs), so they sprayed something down her throat to numb the muscles, and were then able to push the tube down more easily.

Anita knew when people came in to see her, who they were and what they were doing. Although her physical eyes were closed, she seemed to be acutely aware of every minute detail that was taking place around her and beyond. The sharpness of her perception was even more intense than if she would been awake and using her physical senses. She seemed to just know and understand everything—not only what was going on around her, but also what everyone was feeling, as though she were able to see and feel through each person. She was able to sense their fears, their hopelessness, and their resignation to her situation.

Danny and Mum looked so sad and frightened. She wished they could know that she is no longer in pain—she wished she could tell them. "Mum, please don't cry! I'm fine! I'm right here. I'm with you now!"

"I can't find her veins!" I heard one of the nurses saying frantically to the doctor on duty. There was fear in that voice. "They've completely retracted. Oh, just look at her limbs! There's no flesh on them. Her body hasn't been absorbing nutrition for a while." Anita clearly recalled that this was a male voice—a male nurse. He sounded so hopeless, Anita thought. "He's ready to give up on me, and I don't blame him."

"Her lungs are filled with liquid. She's drowning in her own fluid. I'll have to tap it out of her lungs so that she can at least start to breath with more ease." That was the senior oncologist speaking. Anita watched as they worked with great purpose over her motionless body—a form that seemed too small to contain how she was feeling about herself in that moment.

Although the medical team moved with great speed, and there was a sense of urgency in their actions, Anita also sensed an air of acceptance, as though they'd come to terms with the fact that it was too late to change her fate. She was extremely aware of every detail, but she couldn't physically feel anything—anything, that is, except a release and a level of freedom she would have never known before.

"Wow, this is incredible!" She felt so free and light! What's going on? She had never felt this good! There are no more tubes, no more wheelchair. She can move around freely now without any help! And her breathing is no longer labored—how amazing this is?

Anita felt no emotional attachment to her seemingly lifeless body as it lay there on the hospital bed. It didn't feel as though it were hers. It looked far too small and insignificant to have housed what she was experiencing. She felt free, liberated, and magnificent.

Every pain, ache, sadness, and sorrow was gone! She felt completely unencumbered (not having any burden or impediment). She couldn't recall feeling this way before—not ever.

It was as though she had been a prisoner in her own body for the past four years as the cancer ravaged her physical form, and at last she was being released. She was tasting freedom for the first time! She began to feel weightless and to become aware that she was able to be anywhere at any time, and this didn't seem unusual. It felt normal, as though this were the real way to perceive things. She didn't even think it odd that she was aware of her husband and the doctor speaking to each other outside the ICU, some 40-feet-down a hallway.

"There's nothing we can do for your wife, Mr. Moorjani. Her organs have already shut down. She has tumors the size of lemons throughout her lymphatic system, from the base of her skull to below her abdomen. Her brain is filled with fluid, as are her lungs. Her skin has developed lesions that are weeping with toxins. She won't even make it through the night," the man told Danny. This doctor was someone she had never seen before.

Anita watched as Danny's face changed to anguish, and wanted to cry out to him, "It's okay, darling—I'm okay! Please don't worry. Don't listen to the doctor. What they said isn't true! But she couldn't. Nothing came out. He couldn't hear me."

"I don't want to lose her. I'm not ready to lose her," Danny said.

Although she wasn't filled with any attachment to her body, she felt a deep pull on her emotions to the drama that was unfolding around her inert form. More than anything, she wanted to relieve Danny of the deep despair he was experiencing at the thought of losing her.

"Darling, can you hear me? Please listen! I want you to know that I'm okay!" As soon as she began to get emotionally attached to the drama taking place around her, she also felt herself being simultaneously pulled away, as though there were a bigger picture, a grander plan that was unfolding. She could feel her attachment recede as she began to know that everything was perfect and going according to plan.

As her emotions were being drawn away from her surroundings, she started to notice how she was continuing to expand to fill every space, until there was no separation between her and everything else. She encompassed—no, became—everything and everyone. She was fully aware of every word of the conversation that was taking place between her family and the doctors, although it was physically some distance away, outside her room. She knew the frightened expression on her husband's face and could feel his fear. It was as though, in that instant, she became him.

Simultaneously, although she hadn't known of it previously, she became aware that her brother, Anoop, was thousands of miles away on an airplane, anxiously coming to see her. Upon seeing him and his worried look, she once again felt herself being drawn back into the emotional drama of the physical realm.

"Oh wow, there's Anoop! He's on an airplane. Why does he seem so anxious? It looks as though he's coming to Hong Kong to see me!"

Anita recalled feeling his sense of urgency to reach me. She felt an intense rush of emotion toward him. "Oh, poor Anoop. He's worried about me, and he wants to get here before she dies. Don't worry, Anoop. I'll be here for you. You don't have to hurry! I'm not in pain anymore, dear brother!"

She wanted to reach out and give him a hug and assure him that she was okay, and she couldn't understand why she wasn't able to reach out to him. "I'm here, bro!"

She recalled knowing that she didn't want her physical body to be dead before he arrived. Anita was aware of how that would make him feel, and she didn't want him to go through that.

But yet again, as her affection for her brother started to take over and she was becoming overwhelmed with not wanting him to experience the pain of his little sister dying, she found herself being simultaneously drawn away. Each time her emotions took over the situation, she discovered herself starting to expand again, and she felt a release from all attachment. Once more, she was surrounded by the reassuring feeling of a greater tapestry unfolding, where everything was exactly as it should be in the grand scheme of things.

"The further outward I expanded, the less unusual it felt to be in this miraculous state",—in fact, she had no awareness of it being out of the ordinary. It all seemed perfectly natural to her at the time. She continued to be fully aware of every detail of every procedure that was being administered to her, while to the outside world she appeared to be in a coma. She continued to sense herself expanding further and further outward, drawing away from her physical surroundings. It was as though she were no longer restricted by the confines of space and time, and continued to spread herself out to occupy a greater expanse of consciousness. She felt a sense of freedom and liberation that she had never experienced in her physical life before. She could only describe this as the combination of a sense of joy mixed with a generous sprinkling of jubilation and happiness. It stemmed from being released from her sick and dying body, a feeling of jubilant emancipation from all the pain that her illness had caused her.

As she continued to plunge deeper into the other realm, expanding outward, becoming everyone and everything, she felt all her emotional attachments to her loved ones and her surroundings slowly fall away. What she could only describe as superb and glorious unconditional love surrounded her, wrapping her tight as she continued to let go. The term unconditional love really doesn't do justice to the feeling, as these words have been overused to the point of having lost their intensity. But the physical battle she had fought for so very long had finally released its strong hold on her, and she had a beautiful experience of freedom.

It didn't feel as though she had physically gone somewhere else—it was more as though she had awakened. Perhaps she had finally been roused from a bad dream. Her soul was finally realizing its true magnificence! And in doing so, it was expanding beyond her body and this physical world. It extended further and further outward until it encompassed not only this existence, but continued to expand into another realm that was beyond this time and space, and at the same time included it.

Love, joy, ecstasy, and awe poured into her, through her, and engulfed her. She was swallowed up and enveloped in more love than she ever knew existed. She felt much-more-free and alive than she ever had. As she described, she suddenly knew things that weren't physically possible, such as the conversations between medical staff and her family that were taking place far away from her hospital bed.

The overwhelming sensations were in a realm of their own, and words don't exist to describe them. The feeling of complete, pure, unconditional love was unlike anything she had known before. Unqualified and nonjudgmental, it was totally undiscriminating, as if she didn't have to do anything to deserve it, nor did she need to prove herself to earn it.

"To my amazement, I became aware of the presence of my father", who'd died ten years earlier, and it brought me an unbelievable level of comfort to sense him with me."

"Dad, you're here! I can't believe it!"

She wasn't speaking those words, she was merely thinking them—in fact, it was more like she was feeling the emotions behind the words, as there was no other way of communicating in that realm other than through our emotions.

"Yes, I'm here, my darling, and I've always been here—for you and our whole family!", her father communicated to her. Again, there were no words, just emotions, but she clearly understood.

And then she recognized the essence of her best friend, Soni, who'd died of cancer three years prior. She felt what she could only describe as excitement as their presence enveloped her like a warm embrace, and she was comforted. She seemed to know that they'd been around her for some time, long before she became aware of them, all through her illness.

## 5.6  Anita's Journey Back to Life

Within two days of coming out of the coma, the doctors informed Anita that because her organs had miraculously started functioning again, the swelling caused by toxic buildup had subsided considerably. She was extremely positive and optimistic, requesting that the doctors remove the food-tube because she was ready to eat independently. One of her oncologists protested, claiming that she was too malnourished and her body wasn't absorbing nutrients. But Anita insisted that she knew she was ready for food—after all, her organs were functioning normally again. The doctor reluctantly agreed, saying that if she didn't eat properly, the device was going right back in again.

The food-tube was possibly the most uncomfortable of all the ones connected to her body. It was inserted through her nose and traveled down the back of her trachea into my stomach. Liquid protein was fed through it directly into her digestive system. The presence of this tube made her throat feel parched and dry and the inside of her nose itchy and uncomfortable. She was impatient to get rid of it.

After the tube came out, the doctor suggested to Anita's family that the best solid food for her right then was probably ice cream. Not only would it soothe the abrasions in her throat, it would be easy for her to digest without the added effort of needing to chew. Anita's eyes lit up at the suggestion, and Danny set out to get me a tub of her favorite brand of chocolate ice cream.

When the other oncologist performed his routine checkup, he couldn't hide his surprise. "Your tumors have visibly shrunk—considerably—in just these three days!" he exclaimed incredulously. "And the swelling of all your glands has shrunk to almost half their previous size!"

The following day, to her delight, the oxygen tube came out. The doctors tested her and realized she was breathing without any aid, so they removed it. Anita was already sitting up in bed, although her head had to be propped up with pillows because she was too weak to hold it up for any length of time. She was still in really high spirits. She wanted to talk to her family, and she was especially excited to see Anoop (her brother) and catch up with him.

By this point, Anita wanted to listen to her iPod, and she requested that Danny bring it to the hospital for her. Because of all the tubes and wires that were still plugged into her, plus the wound from the skin lesion on her neck, she couldn't wear the earphones. So Danny connected a little pair of speakers and put them on her bedside table so that she could listen to her music.

Because of Anita's euphoric state, she continually wanted to listen to upbeat tunes, although she didn't have the strength in her muscles to even get out of bed, let alone dance. But in her head, she was bopping away happily, and the music helped contribute to her ecstatic mood. At that time, she didn't even fully understand why she was so positive—she just felt that she knew something.

Anita felt like a child. She wanted her music, she wanted to eat ice cream and talk to her family members, and she was laughing and happy. She couldn't get out of bed or move around, but everything seemed perfect in a way she had never experienced before.

Since she was still in the ICU, the doctors decided that she was becoming disruptive to the other patients who were seriously ill! Their family members had started to complain about the music, laughter, and chatter that was coming from her side of the curtain.

"I don't know what to make of you!" Dr. Chan said when he came to see Anita during his morning rounds. "I don't even know what to write in your file. Your case is truly remarkable!"

So on her fifth day in the hospital, she was transferred to a regular room, where she had the privacy to listen to her music and laugh as much as she pleased!

Slowly—very slowly —the understanding of what had happened was coming to Anita. As her mind cleared and she began to remember the details of what had taken place, she found herself wanting to cry about every little thing. There was a tinge of sadness at leaving behind the amazing beauty and freedom of the other realm. At the same time, she still found herself happy and grateful over being back and reconnecting with her family. She was crying tears of both regret and joy simultaneously.

In addition, she felt a bond with everyone in a way she never had before—not only all the members of her family, but every nurse, doctor, and orderly who came to her room. She had an outpouring of love for each person who came to do something for her or take care of her in any way. This wasn't a form of affection that she was familiar with. She felt as though she were connected to them all at a deep level and knew everything they were feeling and thinking, almost as though we shared the same mind.

Anita's bed was next to the window, and shortly after being transferred into the room, one of the nurses asked her if she would like to sit up and look outside. Anita realized that she hadn't seen the outside world for some time, so she felt excited by the prospect and said, "Yes, absolutely!"

The nurse propped her up, and the moment she looked out the window, her eyes welled up. She couldn't keep herself from crying. It hadn't registered until that moment that the hospital was located only a few blocks away from her childhood home in Happy Valley.

As she mentioned earlier, this wasn't where Anit had been going to for her treatments and blood transfusions over the last few years, which was more like a large clinic than a full-scale hospital. The day she went into a coma was the first time she entered the doors of this facility.

So there she was, looking at almost the very same view she had as a child. She could see the horse racetrack in front of the hospital building—and the tram line she had ridden! As she gazed teary eyed at the scenes of her childhood, she felt as though she had come full circle.

Although the view was familiar to her and the scenery was ordinary, somehow the world looked brand-new. Everything seemed so fresh and sharp and beautiful, as though she were looking at it for the first time. The colors were brighter than she knew them to be, and she was noticing every detail as if for the first time. She looked at the surrounding buildings, one of which was the low-rise she grew up in; the park immediately across the street, which she visited when she was little; the trams trundling by; the cars driving past; the pedestrians walking along with their dogs or busily running errands. She saw everything with new eyes, as though she were a child again. The view couldn't have been more ordinary, yet it was the best she had seen in a long time.

# CHAPTER 6

# NEAR-DEATH-EXPERIENCE: SOME MORE TRUE STORIES

## 6.1  Story of Greg Nome

When Gregg Nome was 24 years old, he slipped into the churn beneath a waterfall and began to drown, his body pummeled (struck repeatedly with the fists) against the sandy riverbed. What he saw there surprised him. Suddenly, his vision filled with crystal-clear scenes from his childhood, events he had mostly forgotten, and then he recollected moments from early adulthood. The memories, if that's what they were, were vivid and crisp. Was he reliving them? Not quite. They came at high speed, almost all at once, in a wave. And yet he could process each one individually. In fact, he was able to perceive everything around him: the rush of the water, the sandy bed, all of it brilliantly distinct. He could "hear and see as never before," he recalled later. And, despite being trapped underwater, he felt calm and at ease. He remembered thinking that prior to this moment his senses must have been dulled somehow, because only now could he fully understand the world, perhaps even the true meaning of the universe. Eventually, the imagery faded. Next, "There was only darkness," he said, "and a feeling of a short pause, like something was about to happen."

## 6.2  Greg Nome recounts his Story to Prof. Bruce Greyson

Greg Nome recounted this story at a support group in Connecticut, in 1985, four years after the experience. He had survived, but now he hoped to understand why, during a moment of extreme mortal crisis, his mind had behaved the way it did. The meeting had been organized by Bruce Greyson, now a professor emeritus in psychiatry at the University of Virginia. (Some of the group's members had responded to an advertisement Greyson placed in a local newspaper.) As Nome spoke, Greyson sat, listening intently, nodding along.

Greyson had been hearing of events like these for years. A month into his psychiatric training, in the 1960s, he had been "confronted by a patient who claimed to have left her body" while unconscious on a hospital bed, and who later provided an accurate description of events that had taken place "in a different room". This made no sense to him. "I was raised in a scientific household," he said. "My father was a chemist. Growing up, the physical world was all there was." He felt certain someone had slipped the patient the information. He also thought, "What does that even mean, to *leave* your body?"

For years, Greg Nome tried to put the account behind him, but repeatedly he faced heady stories of people experiencing other-worldly events, either when they had been pronounced 'clinically dead' or thought they were close to it, before being wrestled back to life. In the 1975 best-seller book *'Life After Life*, the psychiatrist Raymond Moody, once a colleague of Greyson's, labelled these episodes "near-death experiences", or NDEs, a term that stuck. "It occurred to me for the first time that this wasn't just one patient," Greyson says. "It was a common phenomenon." He became fascinated by the qualities of the episodes and the questions they raised, including perhaps the biggest of all: what actually happens when we die? "I plunged in," he said. "And here I am, 50 years later, trying to understand."

Prof. Greyson is 74 now. When we talk, he is at home in Charlottesville, Virginia, waiting out the pandemic in a pressed shirt and tie, kind and affable. Over the years, he has collected hundreds of near-death experiences, he says, either from people who, aware of his research, have volunteered their stories, or from patients who happened to have episodes in hospital. In those cases, Greyson's process is nearly always the same: he sidles up to the bedside and gently withdraws information. "I ask: 'What's the last thing you remember before you blacked out?'" he says. "Then: 'What's the next thing you remember after that?' And finally: 'And what do you remember *between* those times?'" Not everyone reacts well to the questions; most people stare at him blankly. "But around one-in-five will say, 'Well, you know, I thought I saw my father, who died 20 years ago,' and I say, 'Tell me about that' – and I let them go…"

Greyson presents his research in a new book, '*After*', which is bound by a series of case studies. The accounts are mystical, like those we know from TV and books, but there are common themes. After a bad reaction to anesthesia, one patient recalled: "I found myself in a meadow, mind cleared, identity intact." The meadow, she went on, was "lit with this glorious, radiant light, like no light we've ever seen," and "a gentle, inner glow shone from each and every plant." Most episodes involve similar feelings of wonder, mental clarity and bliss, Greyson says. Some people recall out-of-body experiences (OBEs), or report travelling through a long tunnel; others meet entities they think of as God or Allah or long-dead family members; some feel time bend and warp, as though it were elastic. Once, a policeman who almost died during surgery asked Greyson: "How do you describe a state of timelessness, where there's nothing progressing from one point to another, where it's just *all there*, and you're totally immersed in it?" Another person recalled: "The energy of my spirit seemed to flow like a great whale gliding through a sea of silent euphoria."

It has been Greyson's role as a psychiatrist to provide a space in which "experiencers" feel comfortable retelling often incomprehensible stories – though even when patients discover the courage to try, they can struggle to find the right language. "When I talk to near-death-experiencers (NDErs), one of the first things they say, is: 'I can't put it into words. There's no way to express this.'" A frustrated experiencer once told him that when he (NDEr) tried to recall events, "I always fall short." Another explained it would be difficult to describe her experience because we live in three dimensions, and what she saw on the border between living and dying seemed bigger somehow. Greyson has found that sometimes people turn to painting or music to recall events, as if true meaning can be shared non-verbally. But even that's insufficient. An NDEr once told Greyson that recalling his near-death experience was like trying "to draw an odor with crayons", which is to say, basically impossible.

## 6.3    Other Experiences mentioned by Prof. Greyson

Given that near-death experiences happen with limited warning, they are almost impossible to test. "We're dealing with a very short space of time," Greyson says. A swimmer is trapped underwater, a roofer falls from a ladder, a bystander, peering down at their phone, is struck by a car. In the book '*After*', Greyson points out that his career has coincided with advances in brain-imaging technology, including the emergence of fMRI scanners, which help neuroscientists observe thinking in action. But equipment like that requires compliance: an appointment is made; a patient agrees to sit still. What happens when an experience occurs randomly, nowhere near a hospital? How do you capture a moment as fleeting and unannounced as the point of near-death?

When Greyson was asked why he decided to publish '*After*' now, after all these years, he explains that "we had to wait until we had enough knowledge about near-death experiences to be able to understand what was going on," by which he means not that we know what NDEs are, but that advances in science have allowed us to rule out a heap of things they are not. "There are physiological hypotheses that seem plausible *theoretically*," he says, but none have stuck. Are feelgood chemicals, like endorphins, released into the body at the point of peril, creating euphoria? Does the brain become starved of oxygen, prompting real-seeming fantasies? Do various areas of the brain suddenly begin to work in concert to create strange, altered states? Nobody knows for sure. "We keep thinking, 'Oh it's got to be this,'" Greyson says. "No, the data doesn't show that. 'Oh, *this* then?' Well, nope, the data doesn't show that, either."

When Greyson mentions his research to his colleagues, he receives "a variety of reactions, from, 'Are you out of your mind?' to

'Oh, let me tell you about my near-death experience.' To formalize NDE research in the 1980s, he developed a survey, the Greyson Scale, which has been translated into over 20 languages and is still in use. (Did you suddenly seem to understand everything? Did you feel a sense of harmony or unity with the universe?) And these has been published widely in respected medical journals. But he can have quirky ideas. In the book '*After*', Greyson writes: "I take seriously the possibility that NDEs may be brought on by physical changes in the brain," though he also accepts that the mind might be able to function "independent" of it. There have been reports of people experiencing near-death episodes while their brains are inactive, he says, and "yet that's when they say they have the most vivid experience of their lives." This doesn't make sense to him. Partway through these conversations, he asks: "Are these the final moments of consciousness? Or the beginning moments of the afterlife?"

These kind of theories put Greyson on wobbly ground among neuroscientists, who mostly agree the mind to be a product of the brain. Of the afterlife, one researcher told him: "This claim is the most extraordinary in science, and there is no ordinary, let alone extraordinary, scientific evidence to support it." (He added: "These are matters of faith.") Another researcher called claims like these "anti-science". One neurologist affiliated with the department of neurology at Copenhagen University Hospital, told him that if "people are able to describe and report their experiences, even many years later", then surely "they have been processed by the brain and stored in its memory centres."

Greyson knows that events in near-death experiences are impossible to corroborate. "We can't do research on a deity," he says, drily. But still, he finds it tough to dismiss wackier theories, even if the data isn't there. When he was asked what his current logical understanding is, he looks resigned. "It seems most likely to me that the mind is somehow separate to the brain," he says, "and, if that's true, maybe it can function when the brain dies." Then he adds, "But if the mind is not there in the brain, where is it? And what is it?"

Near-death experiences are not a new phenomenon. Socrates had one, according to Plato; Pliny the Elder recorded another (in the first century); history is filled with examples of mountaineers falling from cliffs and experiencing bliss rather than terror. But we seem as enthralled now by their meaning as ever, and they continue to be sprinkled liberally across popular culture.

Often we are encouraged to celebrate narratives that promote living the "right" way, which tends to involve appreciating and accepting every moment for what it is, and mindfully placing experiences and relationships above the pursuit of power or prestige or material goods. (Broadly speaking, this is the plot of *Soul*.) Most of us do not live like that, not entirely, and yet we feel like we *should*, lest we waste our precious time on this planet. Which is why near-death narratives fascinating us; and why they persist as events of interest in the culture. They ask: "What would you do with your life, if you had another chance?"

## 6.4    A Report on Three NDE Cases of Hindus

Near-Death experience (NDE) following a severe head injury, critical illness, coma, and suicidal attempt has been reported in this article. Why a few patients report NDE after survival, is debatable though cultural and socio-demographic factors may play a role. In this article, the summary of the features is reported in different stages of NDE by three patients in India, who were seen by the physicians during hospitalization and in follow-up visits with family.

These accounts of NDE in 3 patients of age 30, 22 and 4 years, respectively, have been reported here, who survived a life-threatening condition. A period in which they were unconscious was also noted and considered to be NDE. This was done after recovery from Coma. Interviews were done with the patient and family members about the details of the experience.

### 6.4.1 First Patient

A 30-year postgraduate, Hindu, married woman with a 5-month-old baby, with severe head injury was brought to emergency in Glasgow. She was operated for acute subdural hematoma of left side. She was on ventilator for 8 days and was unconscious for around two months. After this she made gradual recovery over 1 year. During this period of unconsciousness she described that she was in a brilliant light in which she floated. She then went to 'heaven' where there were a variety of Gods with 'hierarchy'. There was the trinity of Brahma, Vishnu and Shiva but even they were in hierarchy 'junior' to 'Om', an apparition of light. She could recall what had been earlier discussed between doctors about technical matters regarding ventilator, endotracheal tube and tracheostomy. Though she was reluctant she was then 'sent back ' by 'Om'. Over the next 7 years she has slowly forgotten most of her description but her belief has persisted.

### 6.4.2 Second Patient

A 22-year-old graduate, Hindu male, suffering from peritonitis had an anaphylactic reaction leading to cardiac arrest for around 10 minutes. He was resuscitated and recovered from this period of unconsciousness in about 36 hours and from sepsis in about 3 weeks. During the unconscious period he described travelling in a tunnel of white light which he was rushing through. He felt a sense of absolute peace and calm during the arrest. He also had an out-of-body experience (OBE) when he observed with detachment from outside, the rush of medicos to resuscitate him. After few months, he could not recall the details other than the light.

### 6.4.3 Third Patient

A 4-year-old male, Hindu child, was brought in hypotensive shock to emergency secondary to gastroenteritis and dehydration. He was pulse-less and unconscious. Over a period of around one week his sensorium improved. After extubating he started describing his experience of being in silvery white clouds with 'time dilatation' or expansion he felt he was there for months although his altered sensorium was for about a week. Subsequently he forgot most of the experience. The response of family members was initially neutral and advised the child not to dwell upon it.

## 6.5   Discussion on these Three NDE Cases

NDE elements include awareness of being dead. OBE in which a person experiences the world from outside the physical body may include moving through a tunnel, communication with light, observation of celestial landscape, meeting with deceased persons, life review and presence of border.

Clinical death is preceded by insufficient blood supply to the brain; because of inadequate blood circulation, breathing, or both is stopped temporarily. If, in this situation, resuscitation is not started within minutes, irreparable damage occurs to the brain and the patient will die. In 1980, a researcher had proposed 5 stages of NDE: (i) peace and contentment, (ii) detachment from physical body, (iii) entering a transitional region of darkness, (iv) seeing a brilliant light, and (v) entering through the light into another realm of existence.

Another researcher had classified NDE into 3 types: (i) out-of-body experience; (ii) transition involving passage of consciousness into a foreign dimension and (iii) the combined experience. NDE survivors have also reported viewing resuscitation efforts from outside, meeting a 'being of light' who helped them evaluate their lives and finally deciding to return to life rather than go into the bliss of death. Vision of Christ and Yama (the God of death in Hindu Pantheon) have also been reported.

Cognitive processes consistent with near-death experiences and resuscitation details from the period of cardiac arrest has been reported by 10-20% of cardiac arrest survivors. Similarly, accounts of children having near death experiences similar to adult have been reported in those who survived cardiopulmonary arrests or coma associated with trauma, hyperosmolar states, or drowning. A similar experience has been reported by a woman who had undergone brain surgery during the period of flat EEG. In cardiac arrest within seconds from the onset of syncope, the EEG usually becomes flat.

Survivors of NDE have also reportedly heard conversations and observed actions of people around them during the time of their comatose state. Furthermore, blind people describing veridical perception during out-of-body experiences in NDE has been reported. Similar experiences, though fragmentary, can be induced through electrical stimulation of temporal lobe during epilepsy surgery, hypercarbia, cerebral hypoxia as in fighter pilots or as in hyperventilation followed by Valsalva maneuver.

A researcher had reported complex hallucinations induced by stimulation of temporal cortex which are perceived as memories by the patient. Yet another researcher reported induced experiences from NMDA receptor blockade and the role of endorphin, serotonin and enkephalin.

Although there are neuropsychological, neurochemical or neurohumoral hypotheses about NDE, yet it is reported to be a non-pathological experience that involves the psychological processes of dissociation as a response to trauma. Depersonalization has also been suggested as a possible explanation in the face of danger. However, in the absence of danger during cerebral ischemia of syncope occasional pleasant feelings and feelings of detachment have been reported.

Other theories of NDE include spiritual theories which presume that consciousness has an independent existence with a belief in after life, or that NDE could be described as birth memories. Yet cultural beliefs and expectations modify the accounts of NDE. A researcher described that sometimes mind can acquire a mental model of reality assumed upon imagery and memory instead of sensory impressions. Plato and other philosophers have proposed many explanations regarding the relationship between perception and reality. Moreover, Darwinian natural selection need not favor veridical perceptions as what matters in evolution is utility and the effects of selection on sensory perception needs study. According to a researcher, a mental state that may be intrinsically quite different from a veridical perception might come to be mistaken for so, and hence gets the status of a hallucination. Accounts of death-bed visions have been consistent with the interpretation as comforting hallucinations with contextual variations. Other studies question the assertion that patients were actually clinically dead and emphasize differences in EEG and variability in brain of each individual. These questions are also pondered by people involved in research in noetic science. However, it gets intriguing when, 'mathematical models' of 'parallel universe' in quantum physics mimic 'experiences' of these patients.

Immense amount of similar literature is reported in Hindu scriptures, like Mahabharat or the Upanishads. Many patients appear to be permanently changed by an NDE which cannot be ignored.

## 6.6   Pam Reynolds' Case of Near-Death Experience

Pam Reynolds Lowery (1956 – May 22, 2010), from Atlanta, Georgia, was an American singer-songwriter. In 1991, at the age of 35, she stated that she had a near-death experience (NDE) during a brain operation performed by Robert F. Spetzler at the Barrow Neurological Institute in Phoenix, Arizona. Reynolds was under close medical monitoring during the entire operation. During part of the operation she had no brain-wave activity and no blood flowing in her brain, which rendered her clinically dead. She claimed to have made several observations during the procedure which medical personnel reported to be accurate.

Within the field of near-death studies and among those who believe in life after death, the case has been cited as well-documented and significant, with many proponents considering it to be evidence of the survival of consciousness after death. An anesthesiologist who examined the case offered anesthesia awareness as a more prosaic and conventional explanation for such claims. Reynolds died from heart failure at the age of 53 on May 22, 2010, at Emory University Hospital in Atlanta, Georgia.

## 6.7  Diagnosis and Operation of Reynolds

Pam Reynolds reported to her physician that she was experiencing symptoms of dizziness, loss of speech and difficulty in moving parts of her body. Her physician referred her to a neurologist, and a CAT scan later revealed that Reynolds had a large aneurysm in her brain, close to the brain stem. Because of the difficult position of the aneurysm, Reynolds was predicted to have no chance of surviving surgery for its removal. As a last resort, Robert F. Spetzler, a neurosurgeon of the Barrow Neurological Institute in Phoenix, Arizona, decided that a rarely performed procedure, known as a standstill operation, or medically induced hypothermic cardiac arrest, could improve Reynolds' chances of surviving surgical removal of the aneurysm. During this procedure, Reynolds' body temperature was lowered to 50 °F (10 °C), her breathing and heartbeat stopped, and the blood drained from her head. Her eyes were closed with tape and small ear plugs with speakers were placed in her ears. These speakers emitted audible clicks which were used to check the function of the brain stem to ensure that she had a flat electroencephalography (EEG)—indicating a non-responsive brain—before the operation proceeded. The operation was a success and Reynolds recovered completely. The total surgery lasted about seven hours with a few complications along the way.

## 6.8  Reynolds Claimed NDE

Reynolds reported that during the operation she heard a sound like a natural 'D' that seemed to pull her out of her body and allowed her to "float" above the operating room and watch the doctors perform the operation. Reynolds claims that during this time she felt "more aware than normal" and her vision was more focused and clearer than normal vision. She reported seeing the surgical "saw" but said it looked like an electric toothbrush, and this is in fact true. She said she could hear conversations between operating room staff, even though she had earphones in her ears which were making a loud clicking noise many times per second in order to monitor her brain function.

At some point during the operation, she says she noticed a presence and was pulled towards a light. She says she began to discern figures in the light, including her grandmother, an uncle, other deceased relatives and people unknown to her. According to Reynolds, the longer she was there, the more she enjoyed it, but at some point she was reminded that she had to go back. She says her uncle brought her back to her body, but she did not want to go, so he pushed her in, and the sensation was like that of jumping into ice water.

## 6.9    Reception After Death and Back for Reynold

Reynolds' near-death experience has been put forward as evidence supporting an afterlife by proponents such as cardiologist Michael Sabom in his book Light and Death. According to Sabom, Reynolds' experience occurred during a period in which her brain had completely ceased to function.

## 6.10    Ninety Minutes in Heaven: A Case of NDE of Don Piper

90 Minutes in Heaven is a 2004-Christian book written by Don Piper with Cecil Murphey. The book documents the author's death and resurrection experience in 1989. '90 Minutes in Heaven' remained on the New York Times Bestseller List for more than five years and has sold over six million copies. The book has also been adapted into a feature-length film, released in theaters on September 11, 2015.

On January 18, 1989, Baptist minister Don Piper was on his way home from a conference in Texas when a semi-trailer truck struck his Ford Escort while crossing a bridge. Piper describes that he was crushed by the roof of his car, the steering wheel impaled his chest, and the dashboard collapsed on his legs. When paramedics arrived, they could not find any sign of life in Piper and covered him with a tarp leaving him there from 11:45 am until 1:15 pm as a fellow pastor prayed over him while waiting for the medical examiner to arrive.

According to Piper, he went straight to Heaven and experienced things he describes as amazing and beautiful, including meeting family members such as his great-grandmother and joining a heavenly choir that proceeded into the Gates of Heaven. Piper, an ordained minister since 1985, has recounted his narrative before 3,000 live audiences that included more than 1.5 million people altogether, and has appeared on numerous television and radio programs.

## 6.11   Near-Death Experience of Eben Alexander

Eben Alexander III (born December 11, 1953) is an American neurosurgeon and author. His book 'Proof of Heaven: A Neurosurgeon's Journey into the Afterlife (2012)' describes his near-death experience that happened in 2008 under medically-induced coma when treated for meningitis. He asserts that the coma resulted in brain death, that consciousness is not only a product of the brain and that this permits access to an afterlife.

Alexander was born in Charlotte, North Carolina. He was adopted by Eben Alexander Jr and his wife Elizabeth West Alexander and raised in Winston-Salem, North Carolina, with three siblings. He attended Phillips Exeter Academy, University of North Carolina at Chapel Hill (A.B., 1975), and the Duke University School of Medicine (M.D., 1980).

Alexander has taught and had appointments at Duke University Medical Center, Brigham and Women's Hospital, University of Massachusetts Medical School, University of Virginia School of Medicine, Boston Children's Hospital, Dana–Farber Cancer Institute et al.

While practicing medicine in Lynchburg at the Lynchburg General Hospital, Alexander was reprimanded by the Virginia Board of Medicine for performing surgery at an incorrect surgical site, two times over the course of a month. In one instance, Alexander altered his operative report because he believed the surgery had diminished the patient's symptoms. He was sued by the patient for damages totaling $3 million in August 2008, but the case was dismissed by the plaintiff in 2009. As a result of the mishaps, Alexander lost his privileges at the hospital and was forced to pay a $3,500 fine to the Virginia Board of Medicine and complete ethics and professionalism training to maintain an unrestricted medical license in the state.

Following the release of his 2012 book 'Proof of Heaven', Esquire magazine reported that Alexander had been terminated or suspended from multiple hospital positions, and had been the subject of several malpractice lawsuits and that he settled five malpractice suits in Virginia within a period of ten years.

Alexander's book(2012) expounds on his near-death experience while suffering from a bacterial meningitis and under a medically induced coma. Alexander describes how the experience changed his perceptions of life and the afterlife. The book was a commercial success but also was the subject of scientific criticism in relation to misconceptions about neurology, such as conflating medically induced coma with brain death.

Alexander presented related lectures around the world in churches, hospitals, medical schools, and academic symposia, besides appearing on TV shows including Super Soul Sunday with Oprah Winfrey. Alexander has also expanded on his NDE in the Congress of Neurological Surgeons and the peer-reviewed Journal of the Missouri State Medical Association. Proof of Heaven was included on The New York Times Best Seller list for 97 weeks.

## 6.12 Pankaj Dheer, an actor for 'Mahabharat' TV show faced NDE

Actor Pankaj Dheer who essayed the role of Karna had faced a near-death experience.

Pankaj faced a new death experience while shooting for a war sequence during B.R Chopra's TV serial 'Mahabharat'.

The team was shooting for the sequence of 'Mahabharat' around Rajasthan in scorching heat. As per the sequence, Pankaj was in a chariot. Reportedly, the Pankaj's chariot was running away in the location and broke mid-way. The horses went haywire but with no time Pankaj acted spontaneously and jumped out of the chariot.

Pankaj Dheer was hit by an arrow near his eye while shooting for Mahabharat and had to undergo the surgery done for the same later.

During the above-mentioned incident in Rajasthan, Pankaj faced a near-death experience.

## 6.13   Near-Death Experience of Murli Menon (in his own words)

*"Nainam chindanti shastrani*

*nainam dahati pavak*

*na chainam kledayanti apo*

*na soshayati marut"*

**Meaning:** Weapons cannot shred the soul, nor can fire burn it. Water cannot wet it, nor can the wind dry it. (Srimad Bhagavad Gita, 2.23)

"Being born into a devout Hindu family whose great granduncle was Swami Tapovan, I was drawn to the Bhagavad Gita like a magnet. The sixth chapter (Dhyana Yoga), always fascinated me but the above shloka in the Gita (2.23) about the soul, had me intrigued. This shloka means, "Weapons cannot cut me, Fire cannot burn me, Water cannot wet me, Air cannot touch me. I am the atman (soul) which is immortal.""

On January 12th 1980 I was flying kites on the terrace of my building at Ahmedabad when due to a quirk of fate, I slipped and plunged feet down from the 6th floor. I hit the floor with a thud; and as a thirteen-year-old, I had my first NDE (Near Death Experience). After three weeks in hospital due to the grace of Lord Brahma,

Vishnu and Mahesh and with the blessings of Goddess Saraswati, Lakshmi and Parvati, I had a miraculous escape and was back to normal except for a few scars on my right foot. I escaped with a fractured ankle and minor bruises.

However, the memory of my first near death experience has stayed with me as if in slow motion and I had realized that the atman is immoral. The Near-Death Experience I underwent had a profound impact on my life and made me extremely spiritual.

I developed a deep interest in numerology and began trying to understand how numbers affected life and how the future could be predicted based on numbers. I passed out of school and college and after graduating in Biochemistry, in 1987, joined a multinational diagnostic company at Kochi for two years, where I purchased my first two-wheeler. I got my first driving license from Fort Kochi and drove for two years in Kerala without accident. I joined another multinational company in a senior position at Bangalore in 1989 and continued to be in Bangalore till 1991. Later I relocated to Ahmedabad as a Product Manager at a pharmaceutical company in 1991 itself.

In 1992 I quit my job and relocated to Pune for my MBA which I completed in 1994. I drove my scooter in Pune for two years without a scratch. After campus placements I joined a Swedish multinational (Astra-IDL, presently Astra Zeneca) at Bangalore as a Product Manager and relocated to Bangalore from Pune on 4th July 1994. Numerologically, my birth year is 1966, so I had my first near-death experience at the age of 14. In 1994, I was 28. On 31st December of 1994, I was returning home on new-year's eve from a party on my scooter, when a drunk truck driver hit my scooter and I had my second near death experience in my 28th year. This accident, caused organic damage to the front temporal lobe of my brain and I slipped into a coma.

The subsequent surgical interventions and craniotomy meant total dependence on powerful antiepileptic drugs for the rest of my life. However after my second Near-Death Experience, I was spontaneously healed and have not had a single epileptic seizure since 1995 till today, though I have gone trekking to Kailash Man Sarovar thrice, Everest base camp, Mount Kota Kinabalu and several unnamed peaks in Uttaranchal, Himachal, Ladakh, Nepal and Tibet since 1995.

Slowly but surely, I recovered from paralysis by combining meditation and NLP (Neurolinguistic Programming) which I was practicing regularly since my first Near-Death Experience. After the first NDE, I had turned vegetarian. After the second NDE, I became a vegan and have strictly abstained from consuming or using any products of animal origin. 14 years later, in 2008, during a visit to Gangotri, I had a spontaneous awakening of my third eye, and started learning Palmistry and Astrology. I started reading palms of total strangers and found that I could narrate the past of total strangers with surprising accuracy. I have retained this gift, since 2008 and have accurately predicted the future of several friends and acquaintances for over a twelve years. As per numerology, I will be completing 14 years since my Ajna chakra awakening in 2008, at the age of 56 in 2022.

After my spiritual awakening and two NDEs, I wrote 20 books on ZeNLP and after publication of my first book titled ZeNLP (Zen + Neuro Linguistic Programming - the power to succeed, started getting invitations from large corporates to conduct ZeNLP based stress Management workshops for their management teams. Since 1995, more than 9000 managers have attended our ZeNLP sessions where we align their soul's life plan with their physical, mental, family and spiritual goals. In the 40 years since my first Near-Death Experience, I had found my mission in realizing the immortal soul for myself and my favorite shloka from the Holy Gita was validated in my NDEs.

The first thing one realizes, when you die, or slip into coma, is that though the body is mortal, the atman is immortal. The atman leaves the body through the Ajna chakra and consciousness remains after death. Post-death consciousness is more vivid than in real life.

One can see colours, unseen during earthly life. One can hear the holy sound OM and the gayatri mantra in afterlife. Consciousness survives death and souls experience an awesome sense of love, connectedness and peace. Just as gravity attracts the physical body downwards, The Hindu cosmic trinity, Brahma, Vishnu and Mahesh combined with the divine feminine (Saraswati, Mahalakshmi and Durga) appear as a beam of dazzling light, brighter than the brightest light on earth, pulls one's consciousness through a divine tunnel. Your whole life flashes in front of you starting from your birth on a cinema-scopic screen, where one's soul experiences, the emotions encountered in our soul's earthly journey.

Before reaching the light, one gets a chance to review one's life from a 360-degree perspective and one realizes how other souls felt during your earthly interactions. You get the chance to experience emotions other souls experienced during your earthly interactions. Love, forgiveness, gratitude and unconditional apologies to souls whom you unknowingly or knowingly hurt including animals, pets, birds and all sentient beings is part of your learning experience on this earthly plane. You must not carry any ill will or resentments or hatred into afterlife, so rather than accumulate karma, it is better to forget, forgive, beg for forgiveness and express gratitude to fellow souls on the earth plane itself rather than in one's life review after death.

After the life review, the Akashic records which track the journey of the soul during Kaliyuga, which started at the death of Lord Krishna are shown by Chitragupta, the record keeper. The more spiritual experiences you have on the earthly plane, the more evolved is your soul. After one analyses one's Akashic records, the choice is yours. You could choose to reincarnate immediately or choose to continue your spiritual learning in the afterlife, with group souls, till you decide to reincarnate to continue your spiritual journey on the earthly plane again. Spiritual development in the earthly plane is much sought after by evolved souls after the Akashic records are studied in-depth.

In 1995, I set 20 impossible goals, while lying paralyzed at a hospital bed at Bangalore after a road accident on New Year's night. My goals included reaching Kailash Manasarovar in Tibet. In 2006, I completed the circumambulation of Mount Kailash. One of my other goals was to take a dip at four consecutive Kumbh melas on the most auspicious days.

Coincidentally, in 2010, I attended the maha Kumbh mela at Haridwar and took a dip in the Holy Ganges on 14th January 2010. In 2013, I reached Prayag raj and took a dip in the holy Sangam of the Ganga and Yamuna. In 2015, I went to Nashik and took a dip in the Godavari during the Kumbh Mela. And finally in 2016, I went to the Shipra River near the Mahakaleshwar temple in Ujjain and took the customary dip in the holy waters of the Shipra. In 2010, I had just landed at Haridwar Railway station where I ran into a two young American girls, with their backpacks. I made small talk with them and found out that they had come from Chengdu in China, where they were teaching English and were going to Rishikesh for a yoga workshop. These two young women, were not aware about the Kumbh mela and its significance. So, I explained to them that they were fortunate to be at the right place at the right time and requested them to join me for a dip in the Holy Ganga at Haridwar on Makar Sankranti, which they did. To my surprise these two American ladies were destined to take a dip in the Ganga and were blessed. After we parted, I realized that these two American English teachers from China were my Group Souls.

Next, at Allahabad Kumbh in 2013, I met a photographer from Delhi who was an alumni of Lady Shri Ram College who had come there to document the Kumbh for a coffee table book for a client. I had randomly requested her to click one of my photographs which she did. And after we started talking, I explained her the significance of taking the holy dip during the Kumbh Mela. It is no coincidence that she accompanied me on the most auspicious day for taking a dip at Prayag raj. She took a dip at the holy Sangam though she had come on an official assignment. I had met another Group Soul.

The same thing happened at the Nashik Kumbh in 2015, where I met two other group souls, in the bus from Shirdi to Nashik. This German couple were backpacking but decided to take a dip in the Godavari on the most auspicious day of the Kumbh Mela in 2015. In 2016, after I reached Ujjain at midnight. from Ahmedabad, all the hotels were completely booked so I had no other option but to sleep on the banks of the Shipra River inside the Mahakaleshwar temple. I slept at the Ghat itself so that I could get up at 2:30 a.m. in the morning and take the customary dip between 3 a.m. and 4 a.m. during the brahma muhurta, which is the most auspicious hour of the day to take chant 9 malas of the gayatri mantra. Each mala contains 108 Rudraksha beads as per Hindu numerology. As soon as I entered the waters of the Shipra-river at 3 a.m. and started chanting, I happened to bump into a group of seven rishis, who were waiting at the edge of the waters!

One by one, all seven entered the waters and I could take a dip with these seven rishis, as I was completing nine dips, because as per Hindu numerology, nine is an auspicious number. This was a dreamlike moment for me. And it was like a dream come true. These seven rishis were again Group Souls and we were destined to meet on at Ujjain in 2016. The goals I had set in 1995, had actualized within 21 years. And I had met ten group souls in the process."

## 6.14 A 60-year-old's Revelation about Return from Death

In a remarkable account, a man, named, Shiv Grewal (a British stage actor), in his 60s faced death on February 9, 2013, as he suffered a cardiac arrest after sharing a meal with his wife Alison near their south-east London residence. Alison quickly dialed an ambulance for help, but it was too late — the thespian's ticker had already ground to a halt. The incident led him to share his extraordinary encounter with the afterlife, providing a unique perspective on the moments following his apparent demise.

Shiv Grewal offered a vivid portrayal of his experience, shedding light on the sensations and revelations that unfolded during the minutes he was declared deceased. Grewal's heart stopped beating by the time paramedics reached the scene in response to his partner's emergency call. Reflecting on the ordeal, he expressed, "I knew, somehow, that I was dying."

Grewal detailed how he felt profoundly detached from his physical body as if he occupied an ethereal void. He recounted experiencing emotions and sensations without the constraints of a human form. Grewal likened this sensation to weightless swimming in the water and revealed, "I walked over the moon and could see meteorites and the whole space." He spent seven minutes in heaven.

"I knew, somehow, that I was dead," Grewal told PA Real Life of the seven-minute experience. "I felt things completely separate from my body. It was like I was in a void but could feel emotions and sensations."

During his other-worldly encounter, Grewal described being presented with a series of options, including various lives and possibilities of reincarnation. However, he steadfastly expressed his desire to return to his earthly existence, emphasizing his longing to reunite with his wife and embrace life again. His account encapsulated the profound choices he faced, underscoring his unwavering determination to continue living in the realm of the living.

The paramedics' timely intervention restored Grewal's pulse after seven minutes of being devoid of vital signs. Urgently taken into surgery, Grewal received a stent to alleviate a complete blockage in his main artery. However, the lack of oxygen during his cardiac arrest resulted in cerebral hypoxia, leaving him with epilepsy. Despite the challenges that ensued, Grewal's experience instigated transformative changes in his life's trajectory.

## 6.15 Near-Death Experience of Indian Actor 'Amitabh Bachchan'

Hindi-Film Hero, Superstar Amitabh Bachchan got injured during the shooting of his movie.

It all happened on the sets of the Manmohan Desai's action-drama '*Coolie*' at Bengaluru. Bachchan was shooting for a high-octane fight scene. One mock punch turned into a fatal blow and led to the megastar fighting for his life at the hospital.

One miscalculated step, that was what nearly sent the dashing six-foot-two-inch-tall 'Angry Young Man' to the arms of death. The stage was set for the showdown in this movie between Iqbal (Bachchan) and Bob (Puneet Issar) the antagonist.

Later on, in his blog, the 'millennium' superstar reminisced about his near brush with death and revealed he had gone into a "coma-like" situation. "I went into almost a haze and a coma-like situation. Within five days of coming into Breach Candy Hospital, I had another surgery and didn't come out of that one for a very, very long time and I was declared 'clinically dead' for a couple of minutes. Then Dr. Wadia, who looked after me and is an absolute life-saver, just said "I'm going to take a last chance" and he started pumping cortisone/ adrenaline injections into me one after another almost, 40 ampules of it, with the hope that something would happen and then I got revived," recalled Bachchan on his blog.

Amitabh Bachchan's injury sent shockwaves throughout the country. Indira Gandhi, the then Prime Minister of India. visited the hospital. Rajiv Gandhi cancelled a tour to the US to be at his side. Thousands of fans lined up at the doors of Breach Candy Hospital to offer blood. According to reports, the star was offered 60 bottles of blood from 200 fans! Prayers and havans were organized across the country for the speedy recovery of the star.

# CHAPTER 7

# OLD TRUE STORIES OF NEAR-DEATH-EXPERIENCES

## 7.1 Old True Stories of Near-Death-Experiences (NDEs)

Through time and across cultures, near-death experiences share common themes and have inspired beliefs about the afterlife.

In 1881, a Native American man named Squ-sacht-un of the Squaxin Island Tribe in Washington territory fell ill and, by all appearances, died. His wife began funeral preparations. As Squ-sacht-un later recounted:

"My breath was out and I died. All at once I saw a shining light – great light – trying my soul. I looked and saw my body had no soul – looked at my own body – it was dead."

His soul, according to one account, had ascended to a house where a man asked him if he believed in God. Inside the house, he encountered a photograph of himself that somehow revealed all the bad deeds he had committed in life. He then witnessed people he knew being burned in a furnace. Ultimately, he met God and was given a choice between returning to Earth to preach Christianity or going to hell. Before awakening, Squ-sacht-un was shown a beautiful, luminescent world where he experienced feelings of peace and comfort. Squ-sacht-un was transformed by the experience, explaining: 'I have seen a great light in my soul from that good land; I have understood all Christ wants us to do. Before I came alive, I saw I was a sinner.'

This is an example of what would later come to be known as a near-death experience (NDE). NDEs have been popularly recognized in the West since the mid-1970s, but people from the largest empires to the smallest hunter-gatherer societies have been having them throughout history. Accounts are found in ancient sacred texts, historical documents, the journals of explorers and missionaries, and the ethnographic reports of anthropologists.

## 7.2 More Old True Stories of Near-Death-Experiences (NDEs)

Among the hundreds texts those of a 7th-century BCE Chinese provincial ruler, a 4th-century BCE Greek soldier, a 12th-century Belgian saint, a 15th-century Mexica princess, an 18th-century British admiral, a 19th-century Ghanaian victim of human sacrifice, and a Soviet man who'd apparently killed himself but was revived during resuscitation experiments. NDEs can happen to followers of any religion, and to those of none.

Descriptions of NDEs from around the world often bear striking similarities to myths of afterlife journeys in different religions. In stories from ancient Sumer and Egypt to India and China and beyond, a soul leaves the body, travels through a dark place to a bright other realm, is greeted by deceased relatives, undergoes some kind of evaluation based on one's life on Earth, meets a deity or other entity that's often described as radiating light, and so on. It's important to keep in mind that these common features are found despite the vast stretches of time and space that separate these cultures.

Not only were these religions grounded in NDEs, they served to democratize NDEs and allow their followers to experience them without having to die

Is it possible that this type of extraordinary experience that is universally associated with nearly dying is a fundamental source of beliefs about the afterlife? For many societies, there's no need to speculate. In historical as well as modern accounts, NDEs are often said to lead directly to new beliefs, including the belief that consciousness can separate from the body and that it continues after death. In more than 70 Native American NDE accounts dating from the 16th-19th centuries, and in more than 20 of them it was stated that the experience was a source of knowledge about the afterlife. Likewise, from the Pacific islands, 19 of the 36 NDE accounts had similar claims.

In a fascinating example from 1634, the Innu of eastern Quebec and Labrador told the French Jesuit missionary Paul Le Jeune that their knowledge about the afterlife came from two of their people who had travelled to the spirit world and returned. Their NDEs empowered the Innu to challenge Le Jeune's claims about the Christian heaven and hell, for, according to the evidence of their people who'd had NDEs, everyone went to the same single realm after death.

NDEs have even been foundational to entire religious movements. Some NDE-based movements promoted a revitalization – a symbolic rebirth – of local culture. A major example is the Ghost Dance religion founded by the Northern Paiute shaman Wodziwob following his NDE and other visionary experiences. But these movements have occurred around the world. In Brazil, Guyana and Venezuela, the Hallelujah religion of the Akawaio people had its origins in the NDEs and visions of its founder. The resulting teachings of such traditions included ritual practices (such as repetitive drumming and dancing, or hallucinogenic drug use) to bring about visionary experiences similar to NDEs. Not only were these religions grounded in individuals' NDEs, they served to democratize NDEs and allow their followers to experience them without having to die.

Some larger religions, such as Pure Land Buddhism in East Asia, valorize NDEs and include numerous accounts of them in their sacred texts. In one example from 705 CE, an assistant governor of the Miyako district of Japan named Hirokuni was apparently dead for four days but then revived. He described how messengers had led his soul across a bridge and took him to a golden palace where he met the king of the other world. He saw punishments being inflicted on his father for his transgressions on Earth, and was told how to avoid such a fate:

"Those who have Buddhist scriptures recited will live in the eastern golden palace and be born in the heaven according to their wish; those who have Buddha-images made will be born in the Western Pure Land of Unlimited Life; those who set living beings free will be born in the Northern Pure Land of Unlimited Life."

Whether such accounts have a basis in any actual historical NDE is unknown, though they do demonstrate how the phenomenon is commonly seen in a religious or spiritual context. As with numerous examples from medieval Europe and from 19th- to early 20th-century Mormons, Hirokuni's story was obviously written to promote religious teachings, for like many people who'd had an NDE, he was reportedly transformed by the experience, and he became a model for pious behavior within his tradition.

It's important to note that NDEs don't always emerge from a religious context, and that their impact on spiritual beliefs is not limited to people who are already religious. Committed atheists can also alter their beliefs and worldviews following an NDE. Upon revival from his NDE, the British logical positivist philosopher A J Ayer allegedly told his doctor: 'I saw a Divine Being. I'm afraid I'm going to have to revise all my various books and opinions.'

Near-death experiences can make it rational to believe in an afterlife while remaining an atheist.

We must also be careful not to overstate the cross-cultural similarities with regard to NDEs. Although they share similar themes wherever they occur, no two NDEs are exactly alike. As with any other experience, they are filtered through our complex layers of culture, language and individuality. Given that he was a converted Christian, Squ-sacht-un's NDE featured Christian imagery and instructions to preach the religion on his return to life. In Eastern examples, people who'd had NDEs are often sent back to the body due to a mistaken identity: the otherworld entities got the wrong person. In Western accounts, however, it is more often in order to complete some Earthly task, such as taking care of a child. One thing the various NDEs have in common, however, is that they're virtually always understood as revealing 'what happens when we die.'

Today, the NDE phenomenon continues to play a major role in our beliefs about souls, bodies, death and beyond. It is both a staple of popular culture and firmly a part of many alternative spiritualities. There are even NDE groups and societies in which members seek to renegotiate their spirituality in light of such experiences. These groups share much in common with religious movements, elevating those who've had NDEs to a higher, often guru-like status, and attempting to codify and disseminate beliefs derived from the experiences. They provide a way for unaffiliated 'spiritual but not religious' people to find a community with certain common beliefs. The testimonies of people who've had NDEs also give comfort to those who grieve the loss of loved ones, and to those who are fearful of death. These benefits come without the attendant commitments and potential philosophical compromises involved in mainstream religious affiliation. After all, believing in an afterlife based on personal experience doesn't necessitate believing in myths of deities and their alleged concern for our daily lives. Near-death experiences can make it rational to believe in an afterlife while remaining an atheist.

There have been many explanations for why people believe in an afterlife at all. Afterlife beliefs have been described as a 'carrot and stick' invention of the ruling class to control behavior with threats of ultimate punishment and promises of eternal reward. Others argue that such beliefs arose from observations of the dying-and-returning cycles of nature – the setting and rising of the Sun, the waning and waxing of the Moon, the annual rebirth of plants and trees. Or perhaps they stem from our yearnings for justice after a life of Earthly disappointments, and are essentially wish-fulfilment fantasies. Most recently, cognitive science has suggested that we're actually hard-wired to intuitively believe in an afterlife.

Each of these theories might play a role in explaining certain aspects of particular beliefs in specific societies. But they all ignore the single human experience most obviously relevant to beliefs in an afterlife: near-death experiences. Whatever the true source of NDEs – biological, psychological or metaphysical – there's no question that they're part of human experience, that they can influence our beliefs about an afterlife, and that they can even contribute to the formation of new religious movements. The phenomenon of NDEs reinforces what humans already seem predisposed to believe: that, in fact, we do not die.

When Squ-sacht-un returned from his NDE, he fulfilled the promise he'd made in the spirit world and began to teach Christianity – though with a markedly Indigenous character. This was the foundation of the Indian Shaker Church, so named because of the ecstatic convulsions of its members during ceremonies. While the Shakers considered themselves Christians, they did not favour the Bible as a revelatory source – relying instead on the testimony of Squ-sacht-un, who was also known as John Slocum. Louis Yowaluch, the head of the Church in 1893, noted the NDE's foundational role in the Church's beginning: 'We heard there was a God from John Slocum. We had never heard such a thing as a man dying and bringing word that there was a God.'

## 7.3  Very Early Reports of Near-Death Experiences

A number of reports from ancient and medieval sources – often couched in terms of mystical or religious visions – have been cited as evidence for NDEs in historical times, yet none of the candidates from classical literature were analyzed at sufficient depth or widely acknowledged by classicists. Notable among these are two Greek descriptions of 'visits to the other world,' which are attributed to two otherwise unknown people identified as Er the Pamphylian and Aridaeus or Thespesius of Soli.

The source for the earlier of these accounts is a speech by Socrates, incorporated in Plato's Republic. Socrates related the fate of "a warrior bold" called "Er, the son of Armenius, by race a Pamphylian", who was left for dead on the battlefield but unexpectedly returned to life at the instant he was placed on the funeral pyre:

"He once upon a time was slain in battle, and when the corpses were taken up on the tenth day already decayed, was found intact, and having been brought home, at the moment of his funeral, on the twelfth day as he lay upon the pyre, revived, and after coming to life related what, he said, he had seen in the world beyond."

In brief, Er reflected that "when his soul went forth from his body he journeyed with a great company," which proceeded towards a meadow portrayed as "a mysterious region where there were two openings side by side in the earth", through which the souls of disembodied people travelled upwards and downwards in space in accordance with the judgment passed on their lives in that place. After an interval of "seven days," they were required to rise up on the eighth and journey on, and they came in four days to a spot whence they discerned, extended from above throughout the heaven and the earth, a straight light like a pillar, most nearly resembling the rainbow, but brighter and purer.

A detailed description of this radiant pillar bears out that it served as the pivot of the cosmos on which the complex movement of the stars and planets as well as the individual fates of living beings depended. The pillar resembled the shaft of a spindle whorl that "turned on the knees of Necessity", a female deity, assisted by the three Fates or Moirai: Clotho, Atropos, and Lachesis. Having then watched how a bevy of souls selected lots for their next lives and drank from a river that erased their memories, Er was suddenly drawn back towards his body and awoke.

The second account examined in this article was reported in Plutarch's The Divine Vengeance in 1984. This account concerned a man from Soli, Cilicia, whose original name was Aridaeus, but who was given the new name of Thespesius in the course of his sojourn in the 'other world.' "He had fallen from a height and struck his neck, and although there had been no wound, but only a concussion, he died away. On the third day, at the very time of his funeral, he revived". Plutarch related that this man, while appearing to be dead, had the sensation that "his intelligence was driven from his body" and that he "had risen somewhat and was breathing with his whole being and seeing on all sides, his soul having opened wide as if it were a single eye". Having familiarized himself with the mobility of his new 'body' and noted the presence of souls of many different types in the elevated environment to which he had ascended, Aridaeus "recognized one soul, that of a kinsman, though not distinctly, as he was but a child when the kinsman died; but it drew near and said: 'Greetings, Thespesius'. This 'guide' then took Thespesius on a tour of the various regions in the 'afterlife.' These regions included "a great chasm extending all the way down … called the place of Lethe" and another "deep chasm in the ambient", which was "a large crater with streams pouring into it, one whiter than sea-foam or snow, another like the violet of the rainbow, and others of different tints, each having from afar a luster of its own". Thespesius also saw a region with "those who were suffering punishment". The "final spectacle of his vision" was that of "the souls returning to a second birth, as they were forcibly bent to fit all manner of living things and altered in shape by the framers of these". While he was watching this scene, a "woman interposed, and he was suddenly pulled away as by a cord and cast in a strong and violent gust of wind upon his body, opening his eyes again almost from his very grave".

A woman who nearly died as a result of a cerebral hemorrhage related: "There was music, very, very pleasant music. The music was beautiful". A young man who tried to kill himself by taking an assortment of pills and, as a result, remained unconscious for four days had a comparable experience: "I also heard music – different music. It was usually like classical music; I like classical music. It wasn't exactly the music I've heard, but it was along that line. It made me relaxed. The fears went away when I listened to it". A woman who "came to this experience as a result, apparently, of suffering cardiac failure at home, where, owing to some unusual circumstances, she lay comatose and undiscovered for three days," then, at a hospital, "had a cardiac arrest before eventually recovering," had memories of "a tremendous rushing sound," somewhat like "the sound of a tornado – a tremendous, gushing wind" and "very high-pitched," followed by music.

## 7.4 A First-Person Account of Near-Death Experience

Here is the first-person account of a person who had near-death experience:

"It was a beautiful August day at Sleepy Hollow Lake in Athens, New York in 1994. The occasion was my in-laws celebrating their annual group birthday gathering. About twenty relatives and their siblings were in attendance. While the children ran amok screaming and playing, I prepared the party barbeque. We had gathered on the second floor of a lakeside pavilion. The ground level included picnic tables and barbeque pits. A payphone was attached to the wall on the side of the building.

As the thought occurred to me to call my mother and check on her, I remember seeing a few light sprinkles of rain. In the midst of the revelry and chaos, and unbeknownst to me, the beautiful sunny day had surrendered to powerful dark storm clouds moving swiftly in over the lake. I ambled around the building to the pay phone and dialed my mother's familiar number. I let the phone ring eight times, but there was no answer. With my left hand I pulled the phone hand piece away from my face to hang it up. When it was about a foot away from my face, I heard a deafening crack. Simultaneously I saw a brilliant flash of light exit the phone hand piece I was holding. A powerful bolt of lightning had struck the pavilion, traversed through the phone striking me in the face, as its massive electrical charge raced to ground.

## 7.5 Another First-Person Account of NDE and OBE

"The force of the lightning blast threw my body backwards like a rag doll. Despite the stunning physical trauma, I realized something strange and inexplicable was happening. As my body was blown backwards, I felt "me" move forward instead. Yet I seemed also to stand motionless and bewildered staring at the phone dangling in front of me. Nothing made sense.

At that moment, I heard my mother-in-law scream from the top of the stairs above me. She raced down the stairs towards me. I felt like a deer in the headlights. As she approached I could see she was looking beyond me to my right and headed that in that direction. She was oblivious to me standing there. I turned to see where she was going. Suddenly, I realized what was going on. A motionless body was lying on the ground some ten feet behind me. To appearances the person was dead. To inspection the person resembled me. To my astonishment another look confirmed it was me!

I watched as a woman who had been waiting to use the phone dropped to her knees and began CPR. I spoke to the people around my body but they could not see or hear me; I could see and hear everything they did and said. It suddenly occurred to me that I was thinking normal thoughts, in the same mental vernacular I had always possessed. At that moment I suddenly had one simple, ineloquent and rude thought, "Holy shit, I'm dead."

This cosmic realization of consciousness meant that my self-awareness was no longer in the lifeless body on the ground. I, whatever I was now, was capable of thought and reason. Interestingly there was no strong emotion accompanying my apparent death. I was shocked, certainly, but otherwise I felt no reaction to what should have been the most emotional of life's events.

Seeing no point in staying with my body, my thoughts then moved to walking away. I turned and started to climb the stairs to where I knew my family still was. As I started to climb I looked down at the stairs like I would normally do. I saw that as I reached the third stair, my legs began to dissolve. I remember being disconcerted that, by the time I reached the top of the stairs, I had lost all form entirely and instead was just a ball of energy and thought. My mind was racing frantically trying to record and make sense of what was happening.

At the top of the first flight, the stairs went up and left into the second flight. Instead of bothering with the stairs, I passed through the wall into the room where everyone was. I went diagonally through the room, over my wife who was painting children's faces. She had one child in front of her, one behind that person and one to the left. I had a clear realization that my family would be fine. Dispassionately, I departed from the building.

Once outside the building, I was immersed in a bluish white light that had a shimmering appearance as if I were swimming underwater in a crystal-clear stream. The sunlight was penetrating through it. The visual was accompanied by a feeling of absolute love and peace.

What does the term 'absolute love and peace' mean? For example, scientists use the term absolute zero to describe a temperature at which no molecular motion exists; a singular and pure state. That was what I felt; I had fallen into a pure positive flow of energy. I could see the flow of this energy. I could see it flow through the fabric of everything. I reasoned that this energy was quantifiable. It was something measurable and palpable. As I flowed in the current of this stream, which seemed to have both velocity and direction, I saw some of the high points and low points in my life pass by, but nothing in depth. I became ecstatic at the possibility of where I was going. I was aware of every moment of this experience, conscious of every millisecond, even though I could feel that time did not exist. I remember thinking, "This is the greatest thing that can ever happen to anyone."

Suddenly, I was back in my body. It was so painful. My mouth burned and my left foot felt like someone had stuck a red-hot poker through my ankle. I was still unconscious, but I could feel the woman who was doing CPR stop and kneel beside me. It seemed like minutes before I could open my eyes. I wanted to say to her, "Thank you for helping me." Nonsensically, all that came out was, "It's okay, I'm a doctor."

Shortly after I regained consciousness, camp security arrived and requested that an ambulance be called, which, to their frustration, I promptly refused. Although I realized I probably made little sense, the truth about lightning strikes is that you are either dead or alive, and there is not much in between. In retrospect it is obvious I wasn't thinking clearly, but at the time, I was still reeling from what I had just experienced. My family drove me the two and a half hours home to Oneonta, NY, wobbly and confused. Once there, I saw my local cardiologist and neurologist who did all the appropriate tests and examinations. They told me how lucky I was to be alive.

I was able to resume work two weeks after the initial lightning strike when my brain seemed to function normally again. In the weeks and months after the lightning strike, however, I changed in many ways. The story of my developing musical ability and composition as a result of this event has been touched on in several books and documentaries."

## 7.6   Introduction to Typical Case Reports of Near-Death Experience in India

Although individual near-death experiences (NDEs) have been reported from India, China, etc., there has been no systematic comparison of the features of cases observed in the West with those observed in another culture. The present report offers as a contribution toward such a comparison. Sixteen Indian cases have been taken for this study.. Of the remaining 16 cases, 10 were interviewed.

All the subjects were Hindi-speaking persons of northern India from Uttar Pradesh and Rajasthan. Eleven were males and five were females. For 14 cases an exact or reasonably approximate age of the subjects was known at the time of their experience; the median age was 35 years. The median interval between the NDE's occurrence and our first investigation of the case was approximately 14 years. The interviews with the subjects and other informants for the cases consisted mainly of recording the principal remembered events of the experience as narrated by the subject or other informant. Afterwards, questions were asked about details, to obtain corroboration for the subject's illness and previous account of his or her experience from whatever other informants. The questions asked of the Indian subjects and other informants (after they had given a spontaneous narrative of the experience) mainly focused on the circumstances of the experience, such as the subject's physical condition, etc.

## 7.7 Some Cases of Mistaken-Identity Reports of Near-Death Experience (NDE) in India

This article reports some features of some cases of mistaken-identity near-death experiences that were investigated in India. After presenting brief accounts of four such experiences, it was observed that the Indian cases differ from a larger sample of American cases. It was noted that some of these features seem to be culture-bound, but it has been cautioned against accepting this observation as adequate evidence that the cases derive only from culture-bound beliefs. Some differences may derive from the effects of a person's beliefs on what actually does happen after death, and some different features may, on closer examination, be found to be basically similar in nature if not in detail.

## 7.8 Four Case Reports of NDE in India

### 7.8.1 Case of Vasudev Pandey

Vasudev Pandey was interviewed, in 1975 and again in 1976. He was born in 1921 and had nearly died in his home, of what he described as "paratyphoid disease," when he was about 10 years old. Vasudev had been considered dead and his body had actually been taken to the cremation ground. However, some indications of life aroused attention, and Vasudev was removed to the hospital where doctors tried to revive him, using "injections," with eventual success. He remained unconscious for 3 days and then became able to describe the following experience:

"Two persons caught me and took me with them. I felt tired after walking some distance; they started to drag me. My feet became useless. Then there was a man sitting up. He looked dreadful and was all black. He was not wearing any clothes. He said in a rage [to the attendants who had brought Vasudev] 'I had asked you to bring Vasudev the gardener. Our garden is drying up. You have brought Vasudev the student.' When I regained consciousness, Vasudev the gardener was standing in front of me [apparently in the crowd of family and servants who had gathered around the bed of the ostensibly dead Vasudev]. He was hale and hearty. People started teasing him saying, 'Now it is your turn.' He seemed to sleep well in the night, but the next morning he was dead."

In reply to questions about details, Vasudev said that the "black man" had a club and used foul language. Vasudev identified him with Yamraj, the Hindu god of the dead. He said that he was "brought back" by the same two men who had taken him to Yamraj in the first place. Vasudev's mother (who had died before the time of our interviews) had been a pious woman who read scriptures that included descriptions of Yamraj. Vasudev, even as a young boy before his NDE, was quite familiar with Yamraj.

### 7.8.2  The Case of Durga Jatav

Durga Jatav, a man approximately 50 years old, was interviewed in November 1979 and again 3 months later. About 30 years before, he had been ill for several weeks, suffering from what had been diagnosed as typhoid. When his body "became cold" for a couple of hours, his family thought he had died. He revived, however, and on the third day following this he told his family he had been taken to another place by 10 people. He had tried to escape, but they had then cut off his legs at the knees to prevent his escape. He was taken to a place where there were tables and chairs and 40 or 50 people sitting. He recognized no one. They looked at his "papers," saw that his name was not on their list, and said, "Why have you brought him here? Take him back." To this Durga had replied, "How can I go back? I don't have feet." He was then shown several pairs of legs, he recognized his own, and they were somehow reattached. He was then sent back with the instructions not to "stretch" (bend?) his knees so that they could mend. (Durga's older sister, whom we interviewed, corroborated his account of his apparent death and revival.)

Durga's sister and a neighbor noticed, a few days after he revived, that marks had appeared on his knees; there had previously been no such marks there. These folds, or deep fissures, in the skin on the front of Durga's knees were still visible in 1979. There was no bleeding or pain in the knees other than the discomfort engendered by Durga's following the "instructions" to keep his knees in a fixed position. X-ray photographs that were taken in 1981 showed no abnormality below the surface of the skin.

Durga had not heard of such experiences before his own NDE. He did not see his physical body from some other position in space. He said that afterward the experience seemed like a dream; nevertheless, he claimed that it had strengthened his faith in God.

One informant for this case (the headman of the village where Durga lived) said that at the time of Durga's experience another person by the same name had died in Agra (about 30 km away); however, neither Durga nor his older sister were able to confirm this statement.

### 7.8.3  The Case of Chhajju Bania

Chhajju Bania was interviewed in 1981, at which time he was about 40 years old. His NDE had occurred some 6 years earlier. He became ill with fever, and his condition deteriorated until he was thought to have died and his relatives began preparing his body for cremation. However, he revived, and he gave the following account of his experience as he remembered it afterward:

"Four black messengers came and held me. I asked, 'Where are you taking me?' They took me and seated me near the god. My body had become small. There was an old lady sitting there. She had a pen in her hand, and the clerks had a heap of books in front of them. I was summoned…. One of the clerks said, 'We don't need Chhajju Bania (trader). We had asked for Chhajju Kumhar (potter). Push him back and bring the other man. He [meaning Chhajju Bania] has some life remaining.' I asked the clerks to give me some work to do, but not to send me back. Yamraj was there sitting on a high chair with a white beard and wearing yellow clothes. He asked me, 'What do you want?' I told him that I wanted to stay there. He asked me to extend my hand. I don't remember whether he gave me something or not. Then I was pushed down and revived."

Chhajju told us that he later learned that a person called Chhajju Kumhar had died at about the same time that he (Chhajju Bania) revived. He said that his behavior had changed following his NDE, particularly in the direction of his becoming more honest.

Chhajju's wife, Saroj, remembered her husband's experience, but her account (to us) of what he told her about the NDE differed in some details from his statement. For example, she said he had told her (after reviving) that at the place to which the four men had taken him there "was a man with a beard with lots of papers in front of him" (not an old lady}. The bearded man said, "His [Chhajju's] papers are not here." After further checking through the papers, the bearded man said, "It is not his turn. Bring Chhajju Kori [a weaver]" (not Chhajju Kumhar). Other discrepancies between the two accounts concerned unimportant details. Saroj remembered her husband telling her that he had not wanted to leave "there" and that he had been "pushed down" before he revived.

### 7.8.4   The Case of Mangat Singh

Mangal Singh, was in March 1983 when interviewed he was 79 years old. He described his NDE, which had occurred approximately 5 or 6 years earlier. Unlike most subjects who have had NDEs, he was not ill at the time or at any rate did not consider himself to be so. He gave the following description of his experience:

"I was lying down on a cot when two people came, lifted me up, and took me along. I heard a hissing sound, but I couldn't see anything. Then I came to a gate. There was grass, and the ground seemed to be sloping. A man was there, and he reprimanded the men who had brought me: "Why have you brought the wrong person? Why have you not brought the man you had been sent for?" The two men [who had brought Mangal] ran away, and the senior man said, 'You go back.' Suddenly I saw two big pots of boiling water, although there was no fire, no firewood, and no fireplace. Then the man pushed me with his hand and said, 'You had better hurry up and go back.' When he touched me, I suddenly became aware of how hot his hand was. Then I realized why the pots were boiling. The heat was coming from his hands. Suddenly I regained consciousness, and I had a severe burning sensation in my left arm."

The area developed the appearance of a boil. Mangal showed it to a doctor, who applied some ointment. The area healed within 3 days but left a residual mark on the left arm, which we examined.

In response to the questions, Mangal said that he thought that he might have been sleeping at the time of the experience, but he was not sure of this. He was unable to describe the appearance of the persons figuring in the experience. It seemed to be less visual than auditory and tactile. He did remember that the senior "official" had picked up a lathi (heavy Indian staff) with which he intended to beat the lesser "employees" before they ran away. Another person had died in the locality at or about the time he revived, but Mangal and his family made no inquiries about the suddenness of this person's death and did not even learn his name.

## 7.9   Additional Relevant Information about NDE in India

Yamraj, the king of the dead, is a well-known figure of Hindu mythology and current Hinduism. So are his messengers, called Yamdoots, and the "man with the book," Chitragupta. Chitragupta's book is conceived as containing a record of all of a person's deeds during the life just ended; judgments from the record determine the assignment of the deceased to heaven or hell until the time for his or her next incarnation. It can be safely assumed that all Indians are familiar with these beings, just as we can assume that nearly everyone in the West has some familiarity with Jesus Christ, the Virgin Mary, and at least a few of the prominent Christian saints, such as St. Francis of Assisi.

Cases of the mistaken identity type appear to occur in relation to the beliefs of the experient, independently of his or her location at the time of the NDE. For example, one of the Indian subjects had a typical mistaken identity type of NDE while he was in Rome. On the other hand, Western persons who have become imbued with Indian religious beliefs may have an NDE showing the influence of the Indian culture. One researcher mentioned, without giving details, the case of a Swedish missionary in India who had an NDE that included the feature of mistaken identity. In another case, an American disciple of Sai Baba (a well-known holy man of south India) had an NDE with one feature often found in Indian cases, that of reading the record of the person's life. The person who had this experience almost died while staying in a hotel in Madras. According to his account later, he found himself (while supposedly dead) standing in a large hall in a "Court of Justice"; Sai Baba was with him. The records of the patient's previous lives were called for; "armloads of scrolls" were brought and read at length. At the end of the reading Sai Baba asked the judge to allow the subject to continue living (under Sai Baba's aegis) in order "to complete my mission of spreading the truth." The judge agreed and the subject then, reluctantly, left the realm where this scene had occurred and returned to his body. Unlike the Indian subjects of these cases (and like many American subjects), this man saw his physical body (as from a position outside it) just before he regained consciousness.

# CHAPTER 8

# CLOSE SHAVE WITH DEATH OF SOME FAMOUS PEOPLE IN THE WEST

## 8.1 Near-Death Experiences of Some Famous People in the West

In the modern age, there are more than ever that celebrities are just like the rest of us. Some are good, some are bad. Some are smart, some are maybe not so smart. But that's to be expected. And just like the rest of us, celebrities have their own brushes with mortality that can occasionally be quite dramatic.

### 8.1.1 Thomas Edison Was Nearly Killed by a Flying Badger

Thomas Edison will forever be known as a prolific inventor and kind of a villain from history. He has been accused of some pretty egregious (shocking) behavior in regards to his infamous feud with Nikola Tesla, not the least of which included electrocuting an elephant. But you can't argue that he wasn't an important figure in history, and his legacy is well secured. And to think, none of it would have happened if a badger had been a few inches closer to him when it exploded.

Back in the day, before he was known as a major inventor, Edison was a train guy. He really liked the train. So much so that he not only befriended train engineers, he got them to agree to what may be the stupidest thing you'll hear all day. They let him ride on the cowcatcher.

If you're not familiar with all locomotives, a cowcatcher was kind of like a metal broom, shaped a bit like an arrowhead, attached to the front of the train. As the name implies, it was ostensibly used to push cows off the tracks. In general, however, it was used to deflect any potential obstacle, thus preventing or at least minimizing damage. It was not a seat.

According to Edison, this was a fine way to travel but for one particular journey. Once, the cowcatcher did its job and hit what he thought was a badger. The result was that the badger was launched toward the locomotive and hit below the headline, adjacent to Edison's head, with "great violence." Edison said he was sitting to one side, so no harm was done. No doubt if it had hit Edison's head, the violence would have been much worse. As a result, Edison had a close shave with the death; though he did not report any near-death experience.

## 8.1.2   Adam Devine Was Nearly Killed by a Cement Truck

Adam Devine has carved a name for himself in comedy, thanks to his hilarious work on Workaholics, not to mention the Pitch Perfect films and The Righteous Gemstones. As funny as Devine is today, his own brush with death was no joke.

Some people say they have near death experiences and mean they were almost hit by a car. Devine was not almost hit by a car. He was hit by a cement truck.

Devine was just 11-years-old and had gone to a store with friends. After waiting for some trucks to pass on the road, he thought the way was clear. But another truck came barreling down the road and hit Devine and his bicycle. He was run under the front wheels and went skidding 500 feet down the street. He says they told him he only lived because his bike took the brunt of the hit.

He broke nearly every bone below his waist and lost much of his skin. They nearly amputated both of his legs, in fact. After being in a medically induced coma for two weeks and undergoing 26 different surgeries over the next few years while he learned to walk again, he was thankfully able to not only recover, but discover his knack for comedy as a way of dealing with his situation. Devine too did not report any near-death experience.

### 8.1.3   Johnny Cash was Nearly Gutted by an Ostrich

Johnny Cash was a man with a reputation. They called him the Man in Black, and he sang the Folsom Prison Blues. He was tough and gritty and a real man's man. He also nearly got taken out by a flightless bird.

In 1981, Cash was at "The House of Cash," his own version of Graceland or the Neverland Ranch. There was a recording studio, a museum, and so on. A big celebration of all things for Johnny Cash. Cash had an exotic animal farm. That included ostriches.

According to Cash, a bad winter had killed several ostriches. When the hen died, her mate became very angry. Cash was just walking the grounds when the ostrich appeared and confronted him aggressively. Nothing came of that and Cash left. But, according to him, the bird was plotting. On his return walk, the bird attacked.

If you've ever seen an ostrich attack, you may not think it's as funny as this sounds at first. It certainly wasn't funny for Cash. Ostriches are basically modern-day velociraptors. Their claws are four inches long. Their kick can disembowel a human and people have needed medical attention for the birds cutting right through to their intestines.

Cash got lucky. The bird's kick broke his lower ribs, and the claw sliced him from his chest down to his belt. He actually attributes the belt with saving his life and preventing the claw from digging deeper and lower. Cash too did not report any near-death experience.

### 8.1.4   Graham Norton was mugged and nearly Bled to Death

Back in 1989, Graham Norton was just a student in drama school when he was mugged at knifepoint. The muggers moved beyond threats and actually stabbed the future actor and talk-show host, in the chest. Although he survived the incident, Norton has also pointed out that it was incredibly serious. In his own words he lost "half" the blood in his body.

According to Norton it was an elderly couple that found him and called an ambulance. At the time, he hadn't even realized he'd been stabbed thanks to fear and adrenaline clouding his senses. It was only when he looked down and saw how much blood he was losing that he realized something very bad was happening. Luckily, he was found in time. Graham too did not report any near-death experience.

### 8.1.5  Hunter S. Thompson nearly killed (but then also saved) Bill Murray

Two actors are most often associated with Hunter S. Thompson: Johnny Depp and Bill Murray. Murray took a stab at portraying Thompson back in 1980 and, to prepare for the role, he got to know the real man. Now if you know anything about both Thompson and Murray, it's that they're unpredictable and a little offbeat. So the two of them together had to be a recipe for something, if not disastrous, then at least memorable.

Murray has said he was hanging out at a pool with Hunter in Aspen. Murray decided to try his hand at a Houdini escape so they tied him to a chair and threw him in the pool. Murray was unable to escape or stand up to breathe, as had been the plan. Luckily, Thompson realized at some point that Murray was not in a good way, so he also saved his life by pulling him out. Murray too did not report any near-death experience.

### 8.1.6  Dolph Lundgren Nearly Killed Sylvester Stallone on the Set of Rocky IV

One of the greatest cinematic matches in history is the bout between Rocky Balboa and Ivan Drago in Rocky IV. Sylvester Stallone's Rocky is representing America and Dolph Lundgren's Drago is a Soviet monster. Unbeknownst to audiences, behind the scenes Lundgren was just as monstrous, though not intentionally.

While filming their legendary fight, Stallone was absorbing some real body blows, take-after-take. He said he felt a burning in his chest after three takes but tried to ignore it. However, later that day when he had trouble breathing he realized something was wrong.

Stallone was airlifted to a hospital and spent eight days in intensive care. As a result of Lundgren's punches, his heart had been rattled around so badly in his chest it began to swell. Had he not sought medical attention the swelling would have increased until it stopped. Stallone too did not report any near-death experience.

### 8.1.7 A Fan Nearly Killed Frank Zappa During a Concert

If you're a Frank Zappa fan, you may have noticed that there's a marked difference between his early recordings and his later ones. His voice changed, and it was a direct result of a surprise attack that occurred when Zappa was on stage in 1971.

A man named Trevor Charles Howell rushed the stage and pushed Zappa into the concrete orchestra pit. The fall was catastrophic and people actually thought Zappa had died. His crumpled body was bent at awkward angles, his neck broken. His arm was paralyzed, he was bleeding from multiple wounds and bones had broken. The reason? Howell's girlfriend had a crush on Zappa.

Zappa ended up in a wheelchair for over a year. His larynx was also crushed in the fall, which resulted in a permanent lowering of the singer's voice. Zappa too did not report any near-death experience.

### 8.1.8 George Lucas Nearly Died in a Car Crash

Love him or hate him, there's no denying George Lucas has been one of the most influential voices in pop culture. The man who made 'Star Wars' has shaped the entertainment landscape in a profound way. And it almost never came to pass.

As a kid, Lucas wanted to race cars. He had a car he had souped up himself and was eager to be a part of that world. Maybe that's what led him and his friends to making, shall we say… less than smart choices. One day while he was in high school, Lucas was racing when his buddy tried to pass him on the left, just as Lucas began to turn. Lucas's car was broadsided and rolled several times as a result, only stopping when it bent around a tree.

Lucas broke bones, bruised his lungs and passed out. He spent a long time recovering and decided maybe race car driving was not for him, instead turning his attention to film. Lucas too did not report any near-death experience.

### 8.1.9 Martin Lawrence Fell into a Coma from Heat Stroke

There was a time when Martin Lawrence was one of the biggest names in comedy. He starred in a hit sitcom and headlined numerous films, including hits like Bad Boys and, of course, Big Momma's House. But Martin has also been known for erratic behavior and questionable choices. One of those choices nearly killed him some years ago.

Stories about exactly what happened are conflicting. Some say Lawrence was running in the actual fat suit he wore in the movie Big Momma's House. Others say he just had on numerous layers. Martin himself told Conan O'Brien that he was trying to lose weight and was wearing a plastic suit. The day was hot and, as a result, he actually passed out from heatstroke. But it was more than that.

As a result of his overexertion, Lawrence ended up in a coma for three days and nearly died. He had been jogging in 100 degrees Fahrenheit heat and as a result, his temperature in the hospital was a staggering 107 degrees. Lawrence too did not report any near-death experience.

## 8.2 More NDE Stories of Celebrities in the West

Invincible as they may seem, celebrities are not immune to fate. Many people have an experience in which, had it not been for x, y, or z, they may not still be here today. Near-death experiences often shape who we are, as they serve as reality checks and reminders that we're only on this Earth for so long. Take a look at the following celebrities who've experienced such, and are wiser for it.

### 8.2.1 Madonna

Amid her 2023 world tour, Madonna was admitted to the intensive care unit for a serious bacterial infection. Though all further performances had been postponed, the superstar made a full recovery.

### 8.2.2 Sharon Stone

Renowned actress and L'OFFICIEL cover star Sharon Stone is no stranger to near-death experiences. As a child, Stone was both struck by lightning a sixteenth of an inch away from her jugular vein. This stream of luck followed the actress into her adulthood, as she later suffered a stroke in 2001. The experience served as the meaning behind her new book 'The Beauty of Living Twice'.

### 8.2.3 Jane Seymour

While on the set of her film 'Onassis: The Richest Man in the World', actress Jane Seymour went into anaphylactic shock after being administered an antibiotic to treat her bronchitis. "You take nothing with you in this life," the actress realized in hindsight. Since then, Seymour has dedicated her life to spending time with her loved ones, determined to not waste her time on this earth.

### 8.2.4 Elizabeth Taylor

1950's Hollywood-favorite Elizabeth Taylor opened up about her near-death experience on 'The Oprah Winfrey Show' back in 1992, nearly 30 years after the occurrence. After falling ill with pneumonia, Taylor underwent surgery and was pronounced dead for 5 minutes. After coming to, the actress claimed she had an out-of-body experience, during which she saw her late husband, Mike Todd, who told her "It's not your time… you have to fight to go back."

### 8.2.5  Demi Lovato

Singer and actress, Demi Lovato has always been vocal about her struggles with addiction. In her YouTube Original docuseries, Demi Lovato: 'Dancing with the Devil', she recounts the fatal night of her relapse in 2018. After six years of sobriety, the singer overdosed on opioids and was found unconscious by her assistant. Had the paramedics shown up just 10 minutes later than they did, Lovato may not have made it.

### 8.2.6  Emilia Clarke

The 'Game of Thrones' actress suffered two brain aneurysms (an aneurysm is a bulging, weakened area in the wall of a blood vessel) in the span of two years. In 2011, Clarke collapsed while working out at the gym, and was later diagnosed with a subarachnoid hemorrhage. After being held in an ICU for a week, the actress recovered. Later in 2013, the actress suffered another aneurysm which required an intrusive surgery that hospitalized her for a month. Clarke's two fatal health scares led the actress to start a charity, 'SameYou', which works to assist those in recovery from brain injuries.

### 8.2.7  Leonardo DiCaprio

Much like his Titanic character Jack Dawson, Leo DiCaprio's had his fair share of travel-related near-death experiences. On a flight to Russia, the acclaimed actor witnessed the engine of the plane blow up upon takeoff, requiring an emergency landing at JFK. The actor has also experienced some close calls due to his thrill-seeking adventures. He had a parachute malfunction while skydiving once and was almost attacked by a great white shark while scuba diving in South Africa.

### 8.2.8  Travis Barker

In 2008, the Blink-182 drummer narrowly escaped a deadly plane crash that killed four other passengers. Barker suffered severe third-degree burns and post-traumatic stress disorder from the accident.

However, two months later, the artist returned to the studio. "It was really exciting to know I still have my chops. It still felt good," Barker told MTV in his first TV interview after the crash. "I still can make it around the kit. Everything felt right, so I'm thankful to be able to play."

### 8.2.9 Liam Hemsworth

Before moving to the United States to start his acting career, Liam Hemsworth grew up in Australia where he regularly surfed with his friends and family. However, there was one time he almost didn't make it back to shore. "When I was a kid, one time I got my leg rope wrapped around my whole body like a ball, underwater," he said of the incident. "Couldn't get up. I was in waist-deep water, but I almost drowned."

# SECTION-III:

## NEAR-DEATH-EXPERIENCE: SCIENTIFIC INTERPRETATION

# CHAPTER 9

# SCIENTIFIC ANALYSIS OF NEAR-DEATH EXPERIENCES (NDES)

The existence of so-called Near-Death Experiences (NDEs), in which dying people report having mystical sensations before being resuscitated, is now widely accepted by cognitive scientists as a respectable research idea. Over the years, various explanations have been put forward for the positive variety of NDEs. Early investigators attached the importance of the transcendental aspects of this experience but these views were challenged by biological explanations. The aim of this article is to evaluate the different interpretations from a biological and parapsychological perspective as well as in the light of the newer observations of particle physics. Selective survey also help to form a framework for future research. Features of cluster analysis and a case example are given. Cultural differences are noted. Biological and transcendental interpretations have obvious pitfalls. An intermediate position is advanced here – that the NDE is a combination of individual hallucination and true extra sensory perception. The current models of mind are inadequate to explain NDEs. Study of NDEs is useful for a deeper understanding of mind. NDEs can be better explained if the existence of an extra-cerebral component is conceptualized in association with the brain even though this non-physical aspect is unobservable with the present-day instrumentation.

## 9.1  Characteristics of the NDE

NDEs are experienced at the moment of imminent or anticipated death but before biological death. They are triggered by various situations such as accident, life-threatening illnesses, suicide attempts and operations or births. Near-Death-Experiencers (NDErs) are quite often 'clinically dead'. Some NDEs occur during an isoelectric ECG or in the mortuary. 37% of NDE-like-experiences occur in non-life-threatening illnesses, and accidents. They are also reported even in psychotic reactions. The earlier research by Raymond Moody created great controversy in thanatology (the scientific study of death and the practices associated with it, including the study of the needs of the terminally ill and their families) as his publishers sensationalized his findings. NDEs typically involve a feeling of deep peace, followed by a sensation of floating through a tunnel towards a bright light - even though NDEs are far from blissful for some people. On cluster analysis, these features can be divided into three groups, namely (i) cognitive, (ii) affective and (iii) transcendental. Cognitive features include distortion of time and a review of one's life or panoramic memory. Affective features are feelings of peace or joy. Visual images of a heavenly world and deceased relatives are common transcendental features. Other frequent elements include buzzing or rushing sounds, feelings of separation from the body, extrasomatic experience or Out-of-Body experience (OBE), passing through a void or tunnel, experiencing a bright spiritual light, encountering a border or a limit and the perception of making a conscious choice or being forced to return to the body. There are cases where normally quiet about their experience; they talk about it only in appropriate situations. 30% of NDErs forget the experience because of the dream-like and dissociative nature of the experience, and the involvement of the amnesia-prone temporal lobe. Some remember it only under hypnosis. NDErs can experience a reverse cultural shock, undergoing a revolution of values and opinions. They develop decreased fear of death and increased conviction of after-death existence. Non-religious people may become religious or spiritually oriented. They develop more sense of responsibility and give more importance to acquiring knowledge. There are psycho-hygienic effects and NDErs have less suicidal inclinations. All true NDErs cherish nostalgia for the experience and find a comfort in it in tough times. A researcher, using a Questionnaire and the previously developed Religious Motivation Scale, found significant differences between the patients who had had an NDE and who had not. The life changes noted included enhanced faith in a supreme power, sanctity of life and a desire for positive human engagement. However, up to a quarter of NDEs are negative. Experiencers of negative NDE also report an OBE and a dark transition zone, and accompanied by unpleasant feelings of fear or panic. They describe encountering bad forces or beings, and entering a hellish environment. But negative NDErs also have a positive life-changing effect. Unsurprisingly, negative NDEs are more suppressed than positive NDErs.

## 9.2    A Case of NDE or NDE-like Experience

The following account of an NDE from a case file has some of the ingredients of an NDE, even though there is no evidence to suggest that the subject had a somatic (relating to the body, especially as distinct from the mind) death but was in a physiological crisis. It is not a classic case of NDE and it is not a case to illustrate that some of the reported cases of NDE are very similar to normal experiences in physiological crisis.

*'I am now an old aged pensioner (aged 77), but over the past years have had occasions of being rushed into hospital, more than once on a 50/50 chance of survival. I would like to relate to one such occasion in particular, where I could say, 'Yes I did have a brush with death, but my experience was so vivid and real, I was totally convinced I had died and returned'. Starting from, when the anesthesian put the needle in the back of my hand. 'Just a little prick', he said, and counted up to ten. I remember 7 or 8. My head seemed to leave me empty – a loud buzzing, then a rushing noise and sound as I went into a dark tunnel. It was like being in an express train, but not literally, as I didn't seem to be enclosed and I could see far ahead and notice the bright light at the end of the tunnel approaching nearer and nearer all the time, although it seemed endless in matter of time. On leaving the 'tunnel', my first impression was that I was in Heaven. But oh dear, it was nothing that I was ever led to believe from all the beliefs and stories. It was so totally unexpected and out of character. The 'beyond' was*

*so flat and massive, no end in sight! No hills or mounds, no buildings of any nature. No trees or gardens of so-called roses, yet it was so tranquil and beautiful. No signs or even a hint of what we have on earth planet. You first step out into space. There is not even ground or earth to walk on; you first float along as a bird would fly. Visions of people were there like a vast community, but there was nothing to touch as they had no material body but masses of colour about their spiritual entity. Each one wore a single long garment in the palest of blues, greens, yellows and purple - there appeared no black or white or even red but all other shades of colour. One couldn't describe the garments as they are not manufactured. Just apparitions swathed in mist like – appearances. They just floated around, like walking on a cloud. There was a delightful scent and odor in the air about them, the place was very calm and peaceful, I felt totally relaxed and happy. I was at rest within myself. Time seemed non-existent. I wanted to stay there, disappointed only because I cannot recollect seeing or meeting any of my family, friends or acquaintances, as on earth. I sincerely did believe they lived on the other side along with our individual and spiritual guides. However I was drawn back to the tunnel, stepped in, and entered. All the emptiness within me seemed to disappear. I had enjoyed the feeling of love and peace and now I was experiencing a sense of life coming back into my body, but could do nothing myself. There were no thoughts, just unexplainable senses that I was aware of. I just floated along again, but had the strange knowledge that I was not on a level, as I seemed to be flying higher and higher upwards - it didn't seem at all like the tunnel I had previously gone down. As I came out of the end of the tunnel, I had the awareness of something or someone gently smacking my face, then heard my name being called out, and on opening my eyes, the light was overpowering and I wanted to close them again, but once more I was smacked a little more roughly and harder and heard the words 'Come on Mr. L -, can you hear me?' Suddenly I realized that I had entered my own physical body! I was back in my hospital bed, alive and back in my ward, and realized or thought it had all been a dream. I have never forgotten that experience and yes, I would say I 'passed over' or had my brush with death but was allowed to return to life and my realities again. But I shall never be afraid of death again; there is nothing to be frightened of anymore'.*

## 9.3    Interpretations of NDEs

Even after a quarter of a century of research into NDE phenomena, there is no consensus of opinion among the scientific community with regard to its interpretation. There are organic, pharmacological, physiological, neurological psychological, socio-cultural, paranormal and spiritual explanations. One researcher considered NDE as a final psychosis where the dying individual acts as his own judge, jury, accuser, prosecutor, defence attorney and witness. He or she alone renders the final verdict of guilty or not guilty. According to the pharmacological view, NDEs are the products of the drugs administered during the illness. However, there are NDE cases in cultures where no advanced modern treatment is available. In India, where patients are looked after at home, there are full-blown cases of NDE. It is argued that psychotropic drugs only interfere with the perception of NDE and block the memories. The physiological view is that NDE is due to the cessation of oxygen to the brain during the clinical death and represents the last compensatory gasp of the dying brain. $CO_2$ accumulation is said to explain the tunnel experience but that does not explain the life review and the Light Beings. NDEs have also taken place when the measured oxygen level was well above the average level. While the possible physiological mechanism underlying NDEs have been speculated upon, there is no research demonstrating the actual physiological conditions associated with NDEs. According to the biochemical view hallucinatory neurotransmitters and endorphins are thought to be responsible for NDEs. So far, no NDE specific transmitter constellations have been detected. Stress-induced limbic lobe dysfunction is a neurological explanation. Another neurological view is that the 'NDE is similar to the autoscopic hallucination. In the OBE, the centre of thinking is in the 'second body' and in the case of autoscopic hallucination the centre of thinking is still in the physical body. Electrical stimulation of the temporal lobe has produced NDE-like experiences. However, visual hallucinations in this situation as well as in temporal lobe epilepsy are mere visual disturbances and not intact visual images as in NDE perceptions. The NDE has also been hypothesized to be a protective mechanism to conserve energy and provide necessary brain stimuli. A researcher identified 288 published cases in which a person claimed to have perceived events at some distant location while in the extra-somatic state. It is also worth mentioning that OBEs have been reported to occur in healthy individuals and under experimental conditions. Depersonalization syndrome occurring at the time of life-threatening danger was another speculation. Psychologists have postulated that NDEs are the product of mental defence mechanisms – denial, dissociation, wish fulfilment, regression and projection. Yet in the NDE, the subject is not escaping from the situation; the patient is frequently witnessing the scene of resuscitation. NDEs have common elements and are independent of the belief system. Even when patients are sure to recover, they may still experience an NDE. The replay of birth experience has been a popular psychological explanation. Regression is used to explain the mystical elements (regression to a state before ego differentiation). But again, the NDE is experienced with an integrated ego identity. The tunnel experience is compared to the birth canal experience. New-born children have very poor perception of objects. But NDErs have full perception of objects. Neither is the birth experience a 'positive' one. People who had Caesarean births also have had NDEs. Tunnel experiences are reported to occur with hallucinogenic drugs, hypnogogic and ecstatic states, argued to be the result of over activity of the visual cortex and not announcing proximity of death. The collective unconscious and the archetypes are used to explain NDE. However, OBEs cannot be explained according to Jungian theories.

Finally, NDEs have been compared to other mental reactions to perceived threat, colored by culture and current stress. None of the organic and psychological theories explain the externally verifiable information the subjects give after the bodily separation. How can some persons who are ostensibly unconscious, if not dead, nevertheless perceive their bodies from above, and sometimes become aware of events occurring outside the reach of their ordinary senses? The biological interpretations do not adequately explain the enhanced cognitive abilities of the NDErs. Parapsychologists believe that enhanced cognitive abilities when the brain is underactive point towards a true involvement of extra sensory perception (telepathy, clairvoyance, precognition). Philosophically oriented investigators think that NDE points towards an intrinsic spiritual reality. They attach even transcendental importance to the reports of Light Beings, making it a symbol of modern mysticism outside the religious field. Recent studies have revealed several features of NDE do not conform to the usual reductionist view. It is stated that NDE can occur when a person is unconscious, which suggests that NDEs may not be purely subjective because in the state of unconsciousness, the modules of the brain responsible for the construction of the world are off-line. There are cognitive scientists who hold the view that NDEs are symptoms of dissociative states or post-traumatic stress disorder. But some other studies suggest that the NDEr's stress response is a normal reaction to an anomalous expression rather than a psychopathological response. Some Swiss physicians claimed to have induced OBE by focal electrical stimulation of the brain of a patient undergoing surgical evaluation for epilepsy treatment, and drew the premature conclusion that the part of the brain that can induce OBE has been located. During the procedure, the patient reported that she was sinking into the bed or falling from a height. The authors report that 'When asked to look at her outstretched arms during electrical stimulation, the patient felt as though her left arm was shortened; the right arm was unaffected. If both arms were in the same position but bent by 90 degrees at the elbow, she felt lower arm and hand were moving towards her face. When her eyes were shut, she felt that her upper body was moving toward her legs, which were stable.' In fact, the experience reported might have been an atypical OBE or OBE-like experience. Electrical stimulation is a mechanism and not a cause and in the case of both intentional and spontaneous OBEs, the cause, that is, the external or internal trigger, is still a mystery.

## 9.4 Death-Bed Visions

There is another body of evidences in thanatology supporting the paranormal components of the clinical death experience. They are described as pre-death visions and are particularly interesting as they occur in full consciousness. These experiences include visions of dead friends and relatives, visions of landscapes from beyond, and heightened sensations of elation or euphoria in the immediate period preceding real death. Some of the ingredients of clinical death experiences are identical to the death-bed visions occurring at the edge of life, which cannot be easily explained away in biological terms. While healthy persons report hallucinations of living individuals, truly dying people claim hallucinations of deceased persons. The visions of dying persons may be considered as a defensive attempt to reduce death anxiety by imagining reunion with familiar persons. However, this view is challenged by cases in which a person near death has reported seeing a recently deceased person of whose death the experiencer had no prior information. Thomas Alva Edison's last words in his death bed were, 'It is very beautiful over there'. He supposedly had other worldly pre-death vision. Fr. Damien of Molokai, who dedicated his life to the outcast leprosy patients from Hawaii, is believed to have had pre-death visions of Jesus and Mary when bystanders noticed that he was staring at a particular spot around his death bed. Death bed visions occur more frequently but less reported even though they provide stronger evidence for post mortem existence. They may be true departing visions, whereas NDEs can be designated only as parting visions.

## 9.5  Shared Death Experiences

Shared death experiences (SDE) are a new addition to survival research. These experiences include persons present at the death of their loved ones experiencing leaving their own bodies, viewing the life review of their loved ones and travelling part-way towards the Light. Such experiences, though common, have been rarely reported in NDE literature. Raymond Moody names these experiences as 'empathic NDEs', 'conjoint NDEs' or 'mutual NDEs'. Like death-bed visions, shared real death experiences could immensely contribute to the evidences for discarnate survival. Two researchers reported a case where the daughter who sat beside her mother's deathbed experienced a 'vision' and during this vision she saw a beautiful garden and hillside from which she saw a dead aunt holding out her hands to her dying mother, and the mother and aunt meeting and going away together.

Raymond Moody recognizes seven elements in cases of SDE: (i) change of geometry, (ii) mystical light, (iii) music and musical sounds, (iv) OBEs, (v) co-living a life review, (vi) encountering unworldly realms, and (vii) mist at death. All the elements are not normally present in the reported cases and a few of the seven elements may be present in individual cases. Moody has recounted his own SDE of his mother in 1994 along with the rest of the Moody family. 'When my own mother died in 2005, my two sisters, who were at her bedside, shared a similar vision during which they saw my deceased brother – who was a professor of forensic medicine – appearing with a smile and taking the hands of our dying mother, both then moving upwards and disappearing from sight'. Shared real death experiences cannot be explained away with the biological interpretations of NDEs. Moody proposes that the 'mirror neurons' of the empathic system might contain the clue to explain the mechanism of transmission of SDE. Dogmatic science may argue that SDEs are merely folie a deux or anecdotal experiences that cannot be replicated

## 9.6   Induced ADCs (After-Death Communications)

After-death communications (ADCs) with profoundly loving experiences may assist the grieving process. Spontaneous ADCs in the form of auditory, visual, tactile and olfactory forms have been reported. ADC is thought to produce psychological reconnection and resolution where traditional grief counselling only helps achieve a level of acceptance of the loss. During a researcher's clinical practice he come across a number of his patients seeking the help of the psychically-gifted to resolve their grief reaction and these professionals' attempt to communicate with the deceased or apparently facilitate the departed to communicating with the loved ones. The Psycho-manteum is a mirror room set up to optimize psychological effects such as trance state. Low light, flickering light and a mirror are key features. Sensory deprivation is helpful for trance induction. The participants first reminisce about the deceased loved ones and gaze at a mirror in such a darkened room. They feel contact from the deceased in the form of messages, visions, touches and a feeling of presence. These experiences do not contribute to evidences of life after death. Raymond Moody uses such rooms as a therapeutic tool to heal grief. One may remember the psychedelic explorers of the sixties who also experienced 'bad trips. Mirror encounters could tear apart some of the unsuspecting explorers. A person experimented with induced ADCs through eye movement desensitization and reprocessing (EMDR) technique. He posits that multisensory ADCs are similar to NDEs. ADCs occur to people who are alive and healthy and who experience another person who has died, whereas NDEs happen to people who are apparently approaching death. The induced ADC experiencers report that they sometimes go through a passageway before they get to the deceased and are loving encounters. They also report beautiful landscapes, but never claim to have come across the 'Light Being' encountered in NDEs. It is argued that the quality and psychological impact of both induced ADCs and NDEs are identical though experienced with different perspectives. One researcher's comparison of NDEs and EMDR-induced ADCs, as well as his assertion that such a treatment modality will resolve the sense of loss associated with grief reaction, has been challenged. However, some theologians who recommend the healing powers of prayer and sacramental nourishment consider ADC through the Psycho-manteum and EMDR-induced ADC, as perverted forms of healing grief and may even label them as black arts. A researcher has made a courageous comparison between visionary experiences with NDErs who describe post-mortem existence consisting of two major divisions, with the possibility of a third division. One of the major division is the 'Cities of Light' with their countryside. The second major division is the 'Realm of Bewildered Spirits'. A third division called 'hell' is suggested by a few NDErs. The distinction between such a realm and the second division is not clear according to most NDErs. The 'Cities of Light' are built of crystal-cool light and appear at different levels, with each city grander than the last one and are characterized by intense level of activity. They are surrounded by countryside with beautiful landscapes of mountains, hills, valleys, fields of golden grass and flowers, meadows, paths, trails, lanes, roads, great forests, brooks, streams, rivers, ponds and lakes. The 'Realm of Bewildered Spirits' is described as a dark, gloomy, and hostile environment where there are millions of unhappy and wicked people who are grey, bewildered, confused, miserable, anguished, dreary, angry and uncommunicative and preoccupied with unresolved problems. Mother Mary has offered information about different forms of discarnate survival through the percipients of apparitional occurrences and has given them glimpses of postmortem conditions of time-fullness where past, present and future are blended harmoniously (Heaven), timelessness, where there are not any changes (purgatory) and eternal damnation, where no changes are possible. Unlike physical personalities who live in the space-time dimension, discarnate personalities trapped in the timeless dimension (purgatory) cannot bring about changes in their personality swiftly and could be trapped in that stage for centuries. There are different levels in this dimension and they tally with a researcher's description of the four locales found in his extra-somatic voyages. The Marian apparition has also reaffirmed the existence of negative and positive entities. All the visionaries were shown Heaven, Purgatory and Hell in visions except some, who did not want to see Hell. Two of the seers, claim that they have been teleported to other realms by the apparition and little one resisted initially having to leave his mother! A researcher records that these two visionaries were bodily transported to these realms, during which they reportedly disappeared for twenty minutes. When they were interviewed, visionary insisted that it was not out of the body travel resulting in paradise-scenes. He also questioned whether such things as OBE really exist, as he had never heard about NDEs. They had experienced a true transportation. None of them claim to have encountered the Light Being or historical Biblical figures. The third division with the features of Hell, a realm described by Marian visionaries, has not been established or delineated in NDE studies. The visionaries assert that this realm has a particular environment and strange people. Some visionaries were shown a vision of Hell and the Marian apparition and made mention of the realm of bewildered spirits and heaven. NDE narrations propose that the level of the dimension the NDEr travels is dependent upon the amount of energy levels and frequencies of light in the spiritual body of the individual and are based on human behaviors while on earth, possibly depending also on the energy level and frequencies of light of the helpers coming to assist their transition. There is indication of a new era in human history, marked by human brotherhood, universal love and peace. A small number of deep NDErs have reported consistently prophetic scenarios for the future of Earth: geophysical changes, meteorological changes, economic collapse and a new era of world peace. The prophetic vision of a period of peace may tally with some other apparitional predictions. Nobody can deny the fact that these predicted events are occurring and others could follow, even though majority of the world community is not cognizant of them.

## 9.7   Cultural Artefacts

Parting Visions are more talked about in the West than in the East. The studies of NDE Researchers now indicate that it is a Universal phenomenon. Western man is educated to be reality orientated right from the cradle and he has been conditioned to experience himself and the events around him as real. Therefore, he is prone to regard his last thoughts as real, whereas oriental people are conditioned to think of the world as unreal (or Maya) and so they might regard their last experiences as also Maya. Culture shapes NDEs, which in turn contribute to the shaping of the culture. In Indian cases, instead of 'Light Beings', they are taken to a Holy Man with a book by functionaries. He discovers a mistake in the book and the individual is asked to return to terrestrial life. Post-NDE marks are found in some Indian cases, branded on their body in the other realm. These residual marks resulted from the subjects being forcefully pushed down (generally those subjects who resisted coming back from the other realm). From the psychological point of view, these marks might have been generated like those of stigmatic, due to autosuggestions or intense concentration on the event on the part of the subjects. No review of a former life is described in NDEs of culture believing in reincarnation and this has been used by parapsychologists to indicate that the concept of reincarnation is a misinterpretation of the contact with the earthly life of another deceased human being. Yet a researcher has found and reported evidence that would make this seem possible, although without claiming he has proved reincarnation.

## 9.8   NDEs and Particle Physics

Scientists failed to offer an adequate explanation for NDEs mainly because all along they were using a material cause to describe what may be an other-worldly phenomenon. The view held by classical physicists that two objects cannot occupy the same space at the same time has been the scientific block to believing in the very existence of a non-physical component in association with the brain, and the same confusion is restricting some NDE researchers in considering non-biological interpretations. This view has been challenged by post-Einstein physicists. **De Broglie's discovery of the wave-like nature of matter can accommodate most of the alleged paranormal phenomenon.**

A researcher (in 2000) stated that two subatomic particles can exist together just as two waves rolling over the ocean heading in opposite directions and passing through each other unhindered, occupy the same area of the water surface. Physics theorizes that all matter, at the basic level, is made up of energy which may be diffused as a field, or condensed as a particle. The discovery of **neutrinos** has made a breakthrough in the thinking of post-Einstein science. These are tiny, subatomic particles without any electrical charges and because they do not couple with electromagnetic forces their presence goes undetected. Most neutrinos pass through the earth unscathed and at typical reactor energies they can travel 25 light years in lead before deflecting. We perceive only when particles in our sense organs are coupled to the particles transmitting particular properties from the object and if there is no coupling, there is no perception. Trillions of neutrinos are passing through one's body every second and yet no one is able to detect them. They pass through matter virtually without our being aware of their presence.

One can only imagine the existence of similar unknown particles not coupled with physical fields, constituting other worlds co-existing with ours. Only the left-handed neutrino (spinning in the counter clockwise direction) can interact through the weak nuclear force with another particle and be detected, while right- handed neutrinos (spinning clockwise) still escape detection - though they may well exist. Right-handed electrons and quarks have been proven to exist. Thus, there may be a variety of neutrino-like particles, in the sense that they are tenuous and imperceptible. It may be conjectured that the extra cerebral component of the 'mind stuff' may be partly or fully composed of such diverse particles. Subtle realms may be made of such 'particle families' coexisting with our physical world without our being aware of their existence. Thus, extra dimensions have been postulated based on elementary-particle physics evidence and the possibility of our consciousness extending to other dimensions has been speculated.

### 9.8.1   String Theory and NDE

**String theory** in physics can accommodate extra dimensions. The three space dimensions that we know are embedded in a 10 or 11-dimensional space-time. In other words, we and all the particles in the standard model are trapped in three dimensions and right-handed neutrinos might be free to roam around the multidimensional Universe escaping detection. Particle physicists are now in a position to consider the tunnel experience more sympathetically as an extra-cerebral experience, accepting the hypothetical existence of the other worlds. While arguing that the mental state or conviction of the scientific investigator influences the behavior of the external world in some instances, a researcher states that other dimensions of the universe exist that are objectively real but accessible only to individuals in specific mental state such as the NDE. NDEs correspond to the quirky nature of wave/particles and the expansion of consciousness observed in NDEs match up to the principles of quantum physics. The concept of 'mental space' is helpful in understanding NDE or parting visions. A person's physical body is in physical space and his mind exists in a personal mental space - a higher dimensional space existing like a satellite spatial system occupied by minds, or at least components of minds. This concept is now supported by particle physics.

Mental events occur in a space that is different from the space we occupy in everyday lives as well from the physical space that physicists describe. For example, the image of a bear that we may hold in our minds (in the absence of a live bear) has spatial dimensions, and we can locate that bear in our minds at a distance from an also imagined river and a salmon in the river at which the bear may seem to lunge. We cannot however speak intelligibly about the distance between an imagined bear and its imagined surroundings, yet we can do so about any object that we locate perceptually in physical space. Mental space is a very personal one and protected from the intrusions of other person's thoughts. A researcher, who supports the aforementioned hypothesis, states that the barriers of the mental space weaken on rare occasions, when we experience unusual telepathy and paranormal communications. The real arena of the NDE is probably in mental space – the complex particle dimension beyond the brain - and it may also be a field of subtle energy system. Weakening of the walls of the mental space may result in getting a glimpse into the locales beyond this subatomic energy system. In the NDE the individual is exploring his own personal mental space fully through the brain and beyond.

## 9.9 The NDE and Lighter Shadow Matter Theory: Two Brains

Some researches – along with the plethora of reported OBEs and NDEs – deserves to be afforded attention by the die-hard skeptical scientists of extra-somatic experiences who dismiss such phenomena. A researcher (1988) made use of the concept of shadow matter in parapsychology, and has brought psychic phenomena within the mechanistic framework. According to his hypothesis, two interlinked brains exist in human beings: first an ordinary matter brain, as described by medical scientists; and secondly a shadow matter brain, made up of shadow matter. The researcher has attempted to explain – mechanistically, rather than neurologically – features of out-of-body experiences and psi phenomena in terms of shadow matter theory. Inspired by the shadow matter theory of astrophysics, it has been proposed that living beings have a twin body that is made up of lighter shadow matter (Shadow Matter Body or SMB) than that of their corporeal presence. Accordingly, OBEs are due to separation of the SMB from the ordinary physical body. The SMB perceives its environment through the detection of s-photons (shadow matter body photons) from ordinary physical objects while having extrasomatic experiences. The detection of s-photons by the SMB is carried out through the SMB's shadow matter eyes that are copies of ordinary eyes. It is contended that similar type of perception takes place in the NDE. Lighter shadow matter hypothesis is a fascinating hypothesis, for this may be the realm where NDEs take place and might explain the lack of direct visualization of NDErs in the OBE state, the NDEr's inability to interact with physical objects and the ineffable nature of many NDEs. Accordingly, the shadow matter (SM) theory, at the start of NDE, the subject's SMB splits into two parts. A thin layer remains bound to the top of the ordinary matter body, while the remaining part of the SM body descends down the tunnel that dissociates it from its bonds with the ordinary matter body. The tunnel that is perceived by subjects is the interior human body, through which the shadow matter moves during contraction and expansion. The compression of this shadow matter is due to the release of stored elastic energy. It is elucidated as follows: 'When compression is complete, a reactive event series occurs, with the contracted shadow matter re-expanding and moving up the tunnel towards the thin layer. During this upward movement the thin layer reaches ignition temperatures. It is then perceived by the shadow matter eyes and shadow matter brain of the SMB as the light at the end of the tunnel.' This postulation that the person experiencing the NDE floats freely in the shadow matter ocean has several deficiencies. The incarnate individuals perceived by the NDE subject are hallucinatory figures related by the shadow matter brain, not their discarnate shadow matter bodies. Assuming that this explanation fits the phenomenon, the resulting conundrum may be resolved by integrating the shadow matter speculations with the concept of personal mental space. It is significant that the SMB is surrounded by a personal shadow matter or mental space which is composed of shadow matter that is lighter than the dark matter. This hypothesized personal space must be well insulated from the exterior world as our mental contents and processes are private and – except for occasional incursions and excursions during paranormal experiences in which we engage with other persons – they remain unknown to others. It may be conjectured that SMB is merely floating within this personal shadow matter space once the gravitational bond between the ordinary body and SMB is severed and is capable of exploring the personal shadow matter/ mental space in detail. If the insulation of the personal shadow matter body space weakens, those in the out of the body state might get an opportunity to gain some insight into the region beyond. Reductionists are not able to find a biological origin for the Light Being. Deviating from a transcendental explanation, it may be conjectured that the Light Being encountered by the NDE subject could be one's own spiritual body. At the start of the NDE, a partial split between the spiritual body and the SMB may be brought about. The construction that it is a split within the SMB may be an uneconomical interpretation. In the NDE, the subject is arguably seeing their own spiritual body and their ordinary matter body by way of the shadow matter brain and shadow matter eyes. In a similar way, a researcher after analyzing 102 reports of NDEs, posited that in the NDE one communicates with one's 'high self '- an aspect of the divine rather than transcendental reality. NDEs that incorporate an encounter with the Light Being may offer evidence of the existence of the non-biological component that is the spiritual body. The Light Being may be illustrative of the beauty and strength of the spiritual body and the dignity of human creation. All these events are probably taking place in the personal shadow matter space or in an adjacent shadow matter space, and not necessarily in transcendental space.

The **NDE may be essentially a quantum experience**. The concept of quantum mind makes the interpretations of NDE more complex, and the quantum mind can fool the brain beyond our imagination. As shadow matter is not scientifically proven to exist, it is more comfortable using the term shadow 'matter like-body' rather than 'lighter shadow matter body'. A belief in the spiritual body tallies with the views of a researcher, who hypothesizes that a human being consists of a physical biomolecular body that is closely associated with higher-energy and lower-energy ethereal bodies, higher-energy and lower-energy astral bodies and higher-energy and lower-energy causal bodies. According to this **dark plasma theory** (formerly known as plasma metaphysics) an 'ethereal double' may support the tissues and biochemical activities in the biomolecular body and give it structural integrity. Astral bodies inhabit the astral universe, which has a space-time signature of four spatial dimensions and one time dimension. Causal bodies inhabit the causal universe, having a space-time signature of five spatial dimensions and one time dimension. The causal bodies may be regarded as equivalent to the spiritual body of the faith traditions. While acknowledging the triviality of some mediumistic communications, it is still interesting to note that a non-transcendental explanation of the Light Being is offered in the mediumistic literature. For instance, a researcher wrote: 'But there is a special period when we enter the gallery of memory and the pictures of our earth life pass before us. Then our Spirit (Greater self) is our Judge.' who considers the OBE only to be a retrospective reconstruction based on sensory cues, may be interpreted as obliquely stumbling upon this when she says: 'Perhaps the 'Being of Light' is myself. In fact in any materialistic view of the NDE it simply must be, because there is no other outside force or entity that it could be. Maybe at some level I am or could be magnificent, golden, awesome, loving and unconditionally accepting.' The NDE may also be an experience beyond our quantum mind; while the quantum mind immensely contributes to the whole drama, it may not necessarily extend beyond our own personal spiritual dimension. The NDE may be a personal spiritual pilgrimage within ourselves.

# CHAPTER 10

# NDE AND THE ELECTROMAGNETIC PHENOMENA

## 10.1 Electromagnetic Phenomena Reported by Near-Death Experiencers

Electromagnetic (EM) aftereffects have been reported following near-death experiences (NDEs). These effects include both (a) EM actions, apparent actions by the individual on the surrounding EM environment, and (b) EM reactions, apparent reactions of the individual to the EM environment. This article reports EM aftereffects among 216 NDErs; 54 persons who had been close to death without NDEs, and 150 persons who had never been close to death. NDErs reported both greater EM actions and greater EM reactions than did either comparison group. Among NDErs, those with higher scores on the NDE Scale reported more EM aftereffects. These findings corroborate and suggest the need for controlled experiments to measure the kinds and strengths of EM fields generated or channeled by NDErs, the kinds of EM fields and devices that are affected by NDErs, and the kinds and strengths of EM fields to which NDErs react.

## 10.2 Introduction to EM Phenomena in NDE

Among the physiological aftereffects that NDErs have reported are electromagnetic (EM) phenomena. These effects include malfunctions of electrical devices, both alternating current and direct current (battery-operated), including wrist watches, lights, televisions, radios, computers, appliances, vehicles, and cell phones, in close proximity to NDErs. Although EM effects were rarely reported by early researchers of NDE aftereffects, they have attracted increasing attention in recent years. One reason for this increased notice may be the dramatic proliferation of electronic devices during that period. For example, quartz watches became available in the early 1970s, computers became available to the public during the mid-1980s, and cell phones gained widespread use during the mid-1990s. Although several early researchers reported NDErs' anecdotal accounts of their EM devices malfunctioning and of their unpleasant reactions to EM fields, such reports were difficult to evaluate in the absence of comparison groups because of their frequency among non-NDErs as well. Indeed, some of these phenomena, such as malfunctioning cell phones and computers, are widely accepted by the general public as facts of life with modern technology. These early reports of EM effects following NDEs raised several questions: First, if NDErs do indeed report EM effects more frequently than do other people, is that increased incidence associated specifically with an NDE or might it be related to coming close to death, whether or not the close brush included an NDE? Second, if NDErs more frequently report EM effects, has the increase manifested only since the NDE, or might it have preceded the experience? And third, if only some NDErs report increased EM effects, what might be the relationship between nature and/or depth of NDEs and increased EM effects? One researcher reported the first controlled study of EM effects, comparing 74 NDErs and 54 people who were interested in NDEs but had not had one themselves, with regard to electric or electronic devices (e.g., car batteries or electrical system, lights, watches, tape recorders, computers, etc.) malfunctioning in their presence. Whereas 24% of NDErs endorsed the item, only 7% of non-NDErs did, a significant difference. The participants provided several narrative comments, such as the following: "I have a difficult time as many computers malfunction and lights will blow when I walk under them. This has happened for years, and I tried to ignore that this was happening. I simply cannot wear a watch for long before it breaks down. I went to a department store and walked in front of their brand-new computer and it stopped working. When I held a fluorescent light in my hands, the entire bulb lit up, like it was turned on. It seemed like there was a lot of static electricity.

The incidents in NDErs included interference primarily with wrist watches, light bulbs, and car batteries. Since that time, NDErs have reported influencing modems, fax machines, satellite radios, televisions, videocassette recorders, intercoms, vacuum cleaners, toasters, airplanes, implantable defibrillators, GPS devices, and Wii consoles. One of the most corroborated accounts came from the Medical Director of Leesburg Hospital in Gainesville, FL, who had had a childhood NDE. She described her experience with her wrist watches:

"They either go backwards, they stop, or I have to put a new battery in every couple of months. I have had lots of problems with cell phones not working. I have to have them constantly changed out. After I had touched the borrowed cell phone I'm using right now, because I had to send mine into the shop to get it repaired, it just beeps all day long if I touch it until I turn it off. The IT specialists at work would tell me I had too much static; so, I actually used static mats; I actually have something on my keyboard before I even touch my computer. Having gone through 6 hard drives in 5 years, my employers have spent some money on me to make sure I'm not full of EM energy; but in the same sense it affects everything that I do."

## 10.3   Methodology of Experiments

The sample of 420 participants included 216 persons (51%) who reported having had NDEs that scored 7 or more points on the NDE Scale, and 204 persons (49%) who either denied ever having been close to death or reported an experience near death that scored fewer than 7 points on the NDE Scale (non-NDErs). Of the 204 non-NDErs, 54 (26% of the non-NDErs; 13% of the total sample) reported having been close to death without an NDE and 150 (74% of the non-NDErs; 36% of the total sample) denied ever having been close to death. The participants were recruited from three different sources. Among those 143 participants recruited from the pool of persons who had volunteered to share their accounts of a brush with death, 91% had had NDEs and 9% had not. Among those 72 recruited from Friends of IANDS groups, 76% had had NDEs, 4%

had been close to death without NDEs, and 19% had never been close to death. Among the 205 online survey respondents, 15% had had NDEs, 19% had been close to death without NDEs, and 66% had never been close to death. Looking at the participants another way, among those 216 who had had NDEs, 60% came from the pool of persons who had volunteered to share their experiences close to death, 26% were recruited from Friends of IANDS groups, and 14% were online survey respondents. Among those 54 who had been close to death without NDEs, 24% came from the pool of persons who had volunteered to share their experiences close to death, 6% were recruited from Friends of IANDS groups, and 70% were online survey respondents. Among those 150 who had never been close to death, 9% were recruited from Friends of IANDS groups and 91% were online survey respondents. It was found that the 216 near-death experiencers and the 204 non-experiencers were statistically comparable in terms of gender and education. Among those participants who had come close to death, those who reported NDEs were older than those who did not, and they reported a brush with death longer ago than those who did not; their ages at the times of their close brushes with death were comparable. As required by the definition of group status by NDE Scale score, the near-death experiencers had significantly higher scores (mean = 17.4 ± 6.4) than did the non-experiencers who had come close to death (mean = 2.8 ± 2.2).

## 10.4 Measurements of EM Effect in the NDErs

### 10.4.1 NDE Scale

The NDE Scale, a self-rated, 16-item, multiple-choice questionnaire, was used to assess near-death experiences. It has been shown to differentiate NDEs from other close brushes with death; and to have high internal consistency, split-half reliability, and test-retest reliability over a short-term period of 6 months and over a long-term period of 20 years. A rating-scale analysis established that the NDE Scale yields a unidimensional measure, invariant across gender, age, intensity of experience, or time elapsed since the experience.

Although the NDE Scale was developed as an ordinal scale without quantified anchor points, the fact that it satisfactorily fits the Rasch model suggests that, for all practical purposes, there do appear to be equal distances between the points of measurement that give the scale interval-level measurement properties.

### 10.4.2 Electromagnetic Phenomena Questionnaire

The Electromagnetic Phenomena Questionnaire developed for this study addressed a variety of effects that may or may not be related to EM fields and that have previously been reported by NDErs. It included 38 questions (some of them multi-part) regarding malfunctioning of wrist watches, light bulbs, radios and televisions, batteries, electrical appliances, cell phones, and other electronic devices in the presence of the individual; and sensations of light or color, humming or other noises, vibration or touch, nausea or dizziness, and other sensations that the individual experienced in the presence of external EM fields. Because EM effects have been associated anecdotally with other purported NDE aftereffects such as apparent psychokinesis and healing abilities, which are not clearly related to EM forces, the questionnaire also included questions about "any other new abilities" since their close brush with death, such as positive and negative effect of the individual on other people's emotions or physical symptoms. Respondents were encouraged to supplement their short answers with narrative elaborations or explanations.

## 10.5   Results of NDE and EM Phenomena

### 10.5.1   Electromagnetic Actions

Among the entire sample, apparent EM actions by the individual on the environment were reported by 67 of the 216 NDErs (31%), by 6 of the 54 participants who had been close to death without NDEs (11%), and by 13 of the 150 who had never been close to death (9%). Statistically, NDErs reported significantly more EM actions than did the two comparison groups ($\chi2 = 31.06$, $df = 2$; $p < .001$). This analysis suggested a medium effect. Furthermore, among the NDErs in this study, the mean NDE Scale score among those reporting EM actions was 19.3 (SD = 6.3), and that among those who did not report EM actions was 15.8 (SD = 6.0). Statistically, NDErs who reported EM actions had significantly deeper NDEs than those who did not (t = 4.13, df = 214; p <. 001). Cohen's effect size value (d =. 57) suggested a medium effect.

### 10.5.2  Wrist watches

NDErs reported difficulty wearing wrist watches significantly more often than did the two groups of non-experiencers, with a medium effect. They also reported wrist watches malfunctioning significantly more often, with a small to medium effect. However, the three groups did not differ significantly in terms of specific kinds of malfunction (watches stopping, watches continuing to run but showing the wrong time, and stopped watches restarting), possibly because the sample size for each individual kind of malfunction was too small to detect the effect.

### 10.5.3  Light Bulbs

NDErs reported light bulbs malfunctioning (e.g., blinking on and off or burning out) in their presence significantly more often than did either of the two groups of non-experiencers, with a medium effect. One NDEr wrote: "It's not uncommon for street lights to go out when I walk under them", and he attached to his e-mailed questionnaire a video clip recorded on his smartphone of a street light repeatedly going off and then on again as he walked toward and then away from it. Another wrote: "When I'm upset and I turn on a light switch, there will be a bright flash and the bulb is burned out"; and a third wrote: "I have trouble driving at night because my headlights will start flashing on and off for no reason."

### 10.5.4  Radios and Televisions

NDErs reported radios and televisions malfunctioning in their presence significantly more often than did either of the two groups of non-experiencers, with a medium effect. One NDEr wrote: "The radio will occasionally turn itself on by itself." Another wrote: "A month after my NDE, I got into a friend's car and the radio that hadn't worked for years started to play." A third wrote: "Radios and TVs often change stations or channels when I am enjoying them a lot. It never happens when I don't care what's on, but only when I am intently listening or watching."

### 10.5.5 Batteries

NDErs reported car batteries or other batteries malfunctioning in their presence significantly more often than did either of the two groups of non-experiencers, with a small effect. One NDEr wrote: "My car went dead when I pulled up to my wife's house to discuss our divorce. The doors locked and would not open, and I had to hand crank my moon roof open and climb out of the top." Participants reported batteries draining prematurely in cars, flashlights, cameras, insulin pumps, TV remote controls, clocks, cell phones, and electric toothbrushes; and many reported batteries malfunction, sometimes reversibly, only when they are emotionally stressed.

### 10.5.6 Computers, Tape recorders, and other Electrical Appliances

NDErs reported computers, tape recorders, and other electrical appliances malfunctioning in their presence significantly more often than did either of the two groups of non-experiencers, with a medium effect.

### 10.5.7 Cell phones

NDErs reported cell phones malfunctioning in their presence significantly more often than did either of the two groups of non-experiencers, with a medium effect. One NDEr wrote: "I can't use them because of countless dropped calls, but friends of mine often have unexplained problems with reception only when I'm around."

## 10.6  Electromagnetic Reactions

Among the entire sample, reactions of individuals to the EM environment were reported by 125 NDErs (58%), by 11 participants who had been close to death without NDEs (20%), and by 19 who had never been close to death (13%). Statistically, NDErs reported significantly more EM reactions than did the two comparison groups ($\chi2$ = 85.71, df = 2; p <. 001), suggesting a large effect. Furthermore, among the NDErs in this study, the mean NDE Scale score among those who reported EM reactions was 19.2 (SD = 6.2), and that among those who did not report EM reactions was 14.8 (SD = 5.8). Statistically, NDErs who reported EM reactions had significantly deeper NDEs than those who did not (t = 5.28, df = 214; p <. 001). Cohen's effect size value (d =. 73) suggested a medium effect. When those participants who reported sensing the presence of strong EM fields when others around them did not were asked about how they sensed the EM fields—that is, which sensory modality was involved—they reported several modalities. Visually, participants mentioned seeing white light, "a weird light," halos, waves and undulating forms, and colors becoming blurry. Auditorily, participants mentioned ringing in the ears, humming, and crackling and crunching sounds. Kinesthetically, participants mentioned heart poundings, body vibrating, goose bumps, tingling, physical cringes, "little shocks across my body, with sensations of skin crawling," "feeling like I could tip over," "sensations around my pacemaker," "feeling of a wave going through me," pressure in the forehead, headaches, hairs raising on the neck or arms, cold sensations, and floating sensations. Interoceptively, participants mentioned nausea, dizziness, lightheadedness, and queasiness. Participants mentioned other sensations including pain, shaking hands, dropping things, aromas, a burnt smell, a sweet smell, tastes, "a menthol breath, like peppermint breath," sleeplessness, "a need to eat crunchy things like celery or carrots," anxiety, and agitation. The numbers reporting individual modalities were too small to permit statistical comparisons.

## 10.7    Discussion about the EM Effect

Both EM actions and EM reactions were reported by NDErs in this study three times as often as by non-NDErs, whether or not those non-NDErs had ever been close to death. Furthermore, the deeper the NDE, the more likely one was to report EM actions and reactions. This pattern held true for every kind of EM action or EM reaction probed, as well as for "other EM phenomena" that participants felt did not fit into either category. These findings corroborate and extend prior controlled studies of EM phenomena in NDErs and non-NDErs as well as other researchers' uncontrolled studies and anecdotal reports. Indeed, no researcher who has investigated the question has failed to find more reported EM phenomena from NDErs than from non-NDErs and to find EM effects that increase with NDE depth. This result leads us to suspect that the different frequencies reported by various researchers may have been due more to differences in how questions were asked, rather than to an increase over the years either in actual EM effects or in NDErs' willingness to acknowledge these effects. Most investigators up to this point have developed their own questionnaires to explore EM phenomena, making it difficult to compare prevalence across studies. For this reason, it would be preferable for future researchers to agree upon one standardized questionnaire. As in prior research, EM phenomena in this study were reported overwhelmingly to be aftereffects of NDEs: three-fourths of NDErs noted these phenomena starting only after the NDE, and only 15% noted them prior to the NDE. Some NDErs reported constant EM actions, such as the participant who reported that her presence never opens automatic electric doors like at warehouse stores. On the other hand, other NDErs reported EM effects that appeared to be activated only under stress, such as the participant who reported that she was unable to record songs for her son's funeral. This result raises the question of whether steady and episodic EM effects are in fact different phenomena, or are variants of the same process. Future researchers might investigate this distinction.

## 10.8   Conclusion on EM Effect and NDErs

The findings from this study confirm and extend those from previous research and anecdotal accounts: NDErs report more EM actions on the environment and more reactions to the EM environment than do non-NDErs, both those people who had been close to death without NDEs and those who had never been close to death. Furthermore, among NDErs, the deeper the experience (as reflected in the NDE Scale), the more likely the experiencer is to report EM actions and reactions. NDErs who report EM effects also tend to report environmental effects that are not clearly electromagnetic.

# CHAPTER 11

# BIOLOGICAL, NEUROLOGICAL, PSYCHOLOGICAL, AND SPIRITUAL MODELS TO EXPLAIN NDEs

## 11.1  Biological Models to Explain NDE

The first category of NDE explanations that will be examined are biological models. Biological models call upon the complexity of human physiology to explain the experience. For proponents of biological models, the NDE can be explained purely on the basis of the biological functions of a dying brain. They often invoke such processes as temporal lobe seizures or anoxia as the cause of NDE phenomena.

### 11.1.1  First Biological Model to explain NDE

One such model presented, is based on evolutionary theory and biology. In this theory, two parts of the human brain are distinguished:

(a) An evolutionarily older, reptilian brain located in the pons; and (b) the younger, more complex mammalian brain represented by the cerebral cortex. The researcher explains that the reptilian brain, like reptiles themselves, can function at lower temperatures, with less available energy resources, and under greater duress than the more complex mammalian brain. The mammalian brain, though more fragile, is responsible for overall human consciousness. As the dominant brain, it overrides the subconscious reptilian brain under normal conditions. Because the reptilian brain is so robust, the researcher posits that it might be able to function in states of hypothermia, hypoxia, or other physical distress when the cerebral cortex no longer functions. At those times as well as any other time, when the cortex is dormant (sleep, coma, hypnosis, or psychotic episodes) the reptilian brain could become dominant.

The interaction between the two brains during physical duress is the basis of the NDE. When a person experiences 'clinical death', the cerebral cortex ceases to function. When the patient sees a tunnel with a bright light, it is assumed that some successful effort towards improving the patient's physical condition has been made. This darkness followed by a bright light would represent the cerebral cortex re-initiating and beginning to resume activity. Likewise, the 'life review' would constitute previous memories that flash before the patient as the brain continues to regain function; It is normal to suppose that the memories would begin with the earliest stored ones and continue to the most recent. It is like the common NDE sensation of incorporeality as infant memories, relating it the feelings of an infant during birth who transitions from a cramped and restrictive uterus to the freedom of a new world. He attributes OBEs to the fact that the cerebral cortex would not yet be completely functional, providing the patient with only the sense of hearing. Since no other data is available through sensory input, the brain must create its own picture of reality; thus, it interprets the loss of sensation as an OBE.

In fact, our body is gone from a sensory standpoint because we have no spatial sensory ability, and our rational, conscious mind is also gone. Illusory free-floating becomes possible, if not mandatory, because we have lost all our normal spatial clues.

The fact that many NDErs claim to see deceased friends and relatives who act as their guide is, like the OBE, explained by primitive memories. It is considered that these come from memories of infancy and early childhood in which adults provide love and care. Such memories are normally suppressed by the cerebral cortex, but they reassert themselves in the form of visions when the cortex is only partially functional. The feeling of warmth reported by NDErs is explained as the physical re-warming of the body that accompanies restored cardiopulmonary and respiratory function. It is assumed that 'the being of light or God' represent another reassertion of memories of religious teachings from childhood. Finally, the patient's cerebral cortex resumes normal functioning, represented by a return to the physical body. In this way, the account for NDE phenomenon using only biological factors can be explained.

## 11.1.2 Second Biological Model to explain NDE

Blackmore (1993) presents a very interesting explanation of near-death phenomenon. In her book, "Dying to Live", Blackmore describes each facet of the NDE and provides a thorough biological explanation for them.

This researcher begins by explaining that everything we experience in the world, either internally or externally, is the result of mental models. The brain is constantly collecting input from our senses and arranging it into meaningful data based on our memory, knowledge and experience. She writes, "reality is simply a vast set of mental models"; and one's sense of self is no less constructed than any other facet of reality. She explains that the 'I' that each person assumes to exist is merely a "model of self who appears to inhabit the body and be in charge of it".

According to her, "I am not a special being inside the head directing attention to one thing or another. Rather, 'I' am just one of many models built by this system and 'my' awareness is just a product of the way that system builds its model of reality."

Given this sense of self, this researcher asserts that the stability of the mental models determines one's subjective feeling of reality. Based on sensory input, the system takes the most stable models, i.e., those that most accurately predict actions and promote functioning, and considers those models to represent reality. Erratic, chaotic models are interpreted as fantasy or hallucinations. The NDE seems like a real occurrence because it presents the most stable model of self during the brain's weakened state. For instance, during the OBE phase of the NDE, one perceives oneself to be a spirit or mind absent of a physical body because this model is the most stable in accommodating the lack of sensory input from the impaired physical systems. Thus, biological processes of physical distress cause all of the elements of the NDE, like the tunnel, light, life review, etc., and the system creates a mental model to accommodate them. NDErs may believe that they have traveled out of their bodies, visited spiritual realities and beings, and then returned to their bodies, when in fact the experience only constitutes another of the brain's many mental models.

## 11.2   Neurology of Near-Death Experiences

That NDEs happen isn't in dispute. The sequence and type of events of which they're composed are similar enough among people who report them that NDEs could be considered a syndrome of sorts akin to a disease lacking a known cause. But just because millions of people have experienced NDEs doesn't mean the most commonly believed explanation for them—that souls leave bodies and encounter God or some other evidence for the afterlife—is correct. After all, people misinterpret their experience all the time (an optical illusion representing the most basic example). Without a doubt, many people who report NDEs are profoundly affected by them, but usually more as a result of their interpretation of the experience (i.e., the afterlife is real) than as a result of the experience itself. It turns out, however, that a number of reproducible observations combined with a bit of conjecture yield an entirely plausible neurological explanation for all the reported experiences that comprise NDEs.

Normally 20% of the heart's blood flow is directed to the brain, but that it can drop as low as 6% or so before we fall unconscious (and even at this level, no permanent injury will result). It is further observed that when our blood pressure drops low and we faint, the vagus nerve (a large nerve that connects to the heart) tilts consciousness toward REM sleep—but interestingly in some people not all the way. A number of subjects seem to be susceptible to what he calls "REM intrusion." REM intrusion most typically occurs, when it does, in the transition from wakefulness to sleep. It was found that the functioning of the mechanism that flip-flops people between REM sleep and wakefulness tended to be different in people who reported NDEs. In those people, it was found the switch was more likely to "fragment and blend" between those two states of consciousness (control of our state of consciousness is found in the brainstem and is tightly regulated), causing such people to simultaneously exhibit features of both. During REM intrusion people have found themselves paralyzed ("sleep paralysis"), fully awake but experiencing light, out-of-body sensations, and stunningly vivid narratives. During REM sleep, many of the brain's pleasure centres are stimulated as well (animals that have had their REM regions injured lose all interest in food and even morphine), which may explain the feelings of peace and unity also reported during NDEs.

Neurophysiology can also explain the feeling of moving through a tunnel so commonly mentioned in NDEs. People are well known to experience "tunnel vision" immediately before fainting. Experiments with pilots spun around in giant centrifuges have reproduced the tunnel vision phenomena by increasing G-forces and decreasing blood flow to their retinas (the periphery of the retina is more susceptible to drops in blood pressure than its centre, so that the visual field appears compressed, making scenes appear as if viewed through a tunnel). When special goggles that generate suction were applied to the pilots' eyes to counteract the blood pressure lowering effect of the centrifuge, the pilots lost consciousness without developing the tunnel vision effect—proving the experience of tunnel vision to be caused by decreased blood flow to the eye.

Perhaps the most intriguing aspect of NDEs is how often they're associated with out-of-body experiences. This too, however, turns out to be an illusion. Evidence that out-of-body experiences have nothing to do with souls leaving bodies can be found in the observation that they've also been reported by people just awakening from sleep, recovering from anesthesia, while fainting, during seizures, during migraines, and while at high altitudes (there's no reason to think the souls of people are leaving their bodies during any of those non-life-threatening situations). But the most fascinating evidence that out-of-body experiences are neurological phenomena comes from studies initially performed in the 1950s by a neurosurgeon named Penfield. He was interested in figuring out how to distinguish between normal brain tissue and brain tumors or scars that were responsible for causing seizures. So he stimulated the brains of hundreds of awake patients in an effort to map the cerebral cortex and figure out where in our brains our physical body is represented.

One patient suffered from temporal lobe seizures and when Penfield stimulated the temporoparietal region of his brain, reported leaving his body. When the stimulation stopped, he "returned," and when Penfield stimulated the temporoparietal region again, he left his body once more. Penfield also found when he varied the current and stimulus location that he could make his patient's limbs seem to shorten or create a body double that existed next to him!

In 'The Tell-Tale Brain', V.S. Ramanchandran describes a patient who had a tumor removed from his right frontoparietal region and developed a "phantom twin" attached to the left side of his body. When Ramanchandran applied cold water to his ear (a procedure known as cold-water caloric testing, which stimulates the brain's balance system, known to have connections to the frontoparietal region), the patient's twin shrunk, moved, and changed positions!

Neurologists have since recognized that the temporoparietal region of the brain is responsible for maintaining our body schema representation. When external current is applied to this region, it ceases to function normally and our body schema "floats." Further evidence that this phenomenon is an illusion comes from experiments in which people who've had out-of-body experiences when transitioning from sleep to wakefulness were unable to identify objects placed in the room after they'd fallen asleep, strongly suggesting the picture they viewed of themselves sleeping in their beds was reconstructed from memory. Though no evidence yet exists that low blood oxygen levels cause dysfunction of the temporoparietal region in the same way as does the applied current, this remains a testable hypothesis and the most likely explanation.

In sum then, as an explanation for what actually explains near-death experiences, the REM intrusion hypothesis has far more evidence to support it than does the idea that we actually do leave our bodies when death looms near.

## 11.3  Another Neurological Model to explain NDE

Another model, proposed in 1997, focuses on the action of neurotransmitters in the hippocampus. This researcher explains that most features of the NDE can be induced by administering the drug ketamine. Among the elements mentioned are traveling through a tunnel, entering a light, telepathic exchanges with a God-like entity, life reviews, and the belief that one is dead. To explain this similarity, the researcher highlights the biochemical effects of ketamine on the hippocampus.

To recount some of the physiology of the brain to explain this interaction. The researcher mentions that the large neurons in the cerebral cortex use glutamate as a neurotransmitter. If the brain is flooded with too much glutamate, which is an excitatory substance, then the neurons will die from excitotoxicity. Glutamate excitotoxicity occurs in hypoxia and epilepsy, to name two common examples. How is this process related to ketamine? The researcher explains that ketamine suppresses glutamate, resulting in the bizarre effects of the drug. Since too much glutamate is lethal to neurons, and since the human body possesses so many protective processes, the researcher posits a natural ketamine-like substance that would prohibit excitotoxicity when the brain is flooded with glutamate during physical duress.

This explanation cannot account for all NDEs. It is supposed that the brain's natural ketamine process might work in conjunction with other processes (like hypoxia, temporal lobe epilepsy, reactivation of birth memories, and regression as an ego-defense mechanism) to produce NDEs. Yet it is considered by many to present a very valuable theory of causality for NDEs.

## 11.4   Introduction to OBE and Autoscopy (AS) of Neurological Origin

An out-of-body experience (OBE) may be defined as the experience in which a person seems to be awake and to see his body and the world from a location outside the physical body. A closely related experience is autoscopy (AS), which is characterized by the experience of seeing one's body in extra-personal space. Both experiences are classified as autoscopic phenomena (AP) as, during an OBE and an AS, the experient sees himself as a part of the extra-personal world. Yet, during the OBE, the experient appears to 'see' himself and the world from a location other than his physical body (Para somatic visuo-spatial perspective), whereas the experient during AS remains within the boundaries of his physical body (Physical visuo-spatial perspective).

OBE and AS (OBE/AS) have fascinated mankind from time immemorial and are abundant in folklore, mythology and spiritual experiences. In more recent times, both experiences became a frequent and popular topic in the romantic literary movement of the 19th Century. Reflecting these popular trends, detailed case descriptions and medical reports began to appear. Since then, both experiences have been described repeatedly in patients suffering from neurological or psychiatric disease. Both AP have been related to various neurological diseases such as epilepsy, migraine, neoplasia, infarction and infection and psychiatric diseases such as schizophrenia, depression, anxiety, and dissociative disorders.

Most neurological authors agree that OBE/AS relate to a paroxysmal pathology of body perception and cognition (or body schema). Yet, it is not known which of the many senses involved in body perception and cognition are primarily involved in the generation of OBE/AS. Thus, some authors postulated a dysfunction of proprioception and kinesthesia, others a dysfunction of visual or vestibular processing, as well as combinatory dysfunctions between these different sensory systems. OBE/AS are also known in the healthy population, where they happen generally once or twice in a lifetime and have a prevalence of ~10%. Parapsychological and psychological authors have intensively investigated OBE/AS in healthy subjects based on case collections, surveys and experimental investigations. Whereas, some parapsychological authors suggest that OBE might reflect the projection of a subtle, non-physical aspect of one's personality in extra-personal space and thus an actual separation of the mind from the body, most psychological theories assume OBE to reflect an imaginal experience. Thus, later authors were able to link OBEs to processes of mental imagery and visuo-spatial perspective-taking. It has recently been included this in his classification of OBE/AS in neurological and psychiatric patients.

With respect to the neuroanatomical underpinnings of OBE/AS, most studies found the parietal, temporal and occipital lobe to be involved. Some of these authors have suggested either a predominance of temporal lobe involvement or parietal lobe. Others suggested that both experiences have no precise brain localization. With regard to hemispheric asymmetries, some authors found no hemispheric predominance, while others have suggested a right hemispheric predominance.

Despite these numerous investigations, systematic neurological studies of OBE and AS are rare. To date, there is no widely accepted and testable neuroscientific theory about the central mechanisms of OBE/AS. This is surprising as other body illusions, such as supernumerary phantom limbs or the transformation of an extremity (visual illusions of body parts), have been systematically investigated by many neuroscientists. Importantly, these studies have led to the description of some of the central mechanisms of visual illusions of body parts and to the development of more efficient treatments. However, this is not the case for visual illusions of the entire body such as OBE/AS, which continue to occupy a neglected position between neurobiology and mysticism.

## 11.5 Methods of Research Study for OBE/AS

### 11.5.1 Phenomenology

Each case was analyzed by means of a semi-structured interview, which recorded detailed phenomenological information about the OBE/AS (visual, vestibular, auditory, tactile, proprioceptive and motor characteristics). It was also inquired about the visuo-spatial perspective from which the experience was 'seen' (physical or Para somatic visual perspective) and the visual characteristics of one's own 'seen' body (completeness: whether all body parts were seen; body position: standing, sitting, supine; eventual actions). It was asked explicitly for simple and complex visual, auditory and tactile hallucinations, the presence of visual field loss, and visual and non-visual body-part illusions. With respect to vestibular manifestations, it was inquired about the sensation of rotation, vertigo, falling, elevation, flying, floating, lightness and heaviness. For all manifestations, it was asked whether they appeared before, during, or after OBE/AS or at different instances. Further, it was also inquired about emotional feelings during OBE/AS.

### 11.5.2 Surface and Intracranial EEG, Electrical cortical Stimulation

Continuous long-term video-EEG recordings with 29 scalp and two sphenoidal electrodes were carried out in three patients. Repetitive EEGs in other two patients were performed by 19 scalp electrodes. Patients 2 and 3 were further investigated using subdural grid recordings, since non-invasive investigations did not allow to define the epileptic focus and its anatomical dissociation from vital cortex. Eighty-eight electrodes were implanted in patient 2 and 102 electrodes in patient 3. Subdural electrodes and electrical stimulation were used.

### 11.5.3 Clinical Examination

A complete neurological examination including quantitative visual field testing and an extensive neuropsychological examination (oral and written language, visual gnosis, spatial functions, executive functions, memory; was carried out for each patient.

## 11.5.4   Neuroimaging

In all patients, 3D MRI was carried out. MRI sequences included T1, T2 weighted imaging as well as a fluid attenuated inversion recovery (FLAIR) sequence (additional diffusion and perfusion imaging were performed for patient 4). For each patient, the anatomical region implicated in OBE/AS generation was estimated based on neuroimaging examinations that were available in each patient [in addition to 3D MRI: intracranial EEG, intracranial stimulation, EEG spike mapping, PET and single photon emission computer tomography (SPECT)]. EEG spike mapping was performed by applying a distributed linear inverse solution [LAURA (based on Local AUtoRegressive Averages);] within the 3D MRI of the patient.

## 11.5.5   Individual Lesion Analysis

For each patient, the results of neuroimaging examinations were transformed to the individual patient's 3D MRI. Three-dimensional rendering and superimposing of the individual lesions and localized dysfunctions were carried out using AVS software (Advanced Visual System). In Patient 1, ictal SPECT and three-dimensional EEG spike mapping were matched to MRI (PET could not be recovered in digital format). In Patient 2, the gyral location of the intracranial electrodes where her seizures (those related to OBEs) started, was matched to MRI. In Patient 3, the gyral location of the intracranial electrodes whose stimulation resulted in an OBE was matched to MRI. In Patient 4, no lesion could be determined (MRI and EEG recordings were normal). In Patient 5, diffusion MRI and EEG spike mapping were matched to MRI (neither SPECT nor PET were carried out). In Patient 6, interictal PET and EEG spike mapping were matched to MRI (ictal SPECT was unrevealing).

### 11.5.6   Group Lesion Analysis

The regions as suggested by the individual overlap analysis for the five patients (all patients except patient 4) were used to determine the region of overlap overall patients (mean overlap analysis). This was performed by transposing the MRI (including the location of individual lesion overlap) of each patient onto patient 5's MRI (left hemisphere).

All OBE-patients saw their own body as lying on the ground or in bed, whereas all AS-patients saw their body in an upright position (standing or sitting). These 'seen' own body positions agree with the patient's physical body position prior to the AP. Thus, all three OBE-patients were in supine position prior to their OBE. Patient 1 did not remember her body position prior to the OBEs and stated that seizures could occur in any body position. With respect to body position prior to AS, an initial sitting body position was found for most AS-patients. In Patients 4 and 5, this was observed by the authors directly (Patient 5) or the wife of patient 4.

All OBE-patients experienced vestibular sensations characterized by feelings of flying or floating. Vertigo was rare and reported only by patient 1. Patient 3 also experienced sensations of heaviness and falling. Patients 2 and 3 felt immediately elevated and floating in the Para somatic position, whereas Patient 1 experienced different levels of elevation. There were no reports of actually experienced rotations into the 180° inverted OBE position (along the vertical axis) or rotational sensations along the other bodily axes (binaural axis or axis of sight. Thus, the 180° inversion of the elevated Para somatic body and the elevated visuo-spatial perspective with respect to the extra-personal space and the physical body was always experienced as immediate.

## 11.6   Dissociation of Mind and Body, who have NDE

Some people who come close to death report having experiences in which they transcend the boundaries of the ego and the confines of time and space. Such near-death experiences (NDEs) share some features with the phenomenon of dissociation, in which a person's self-identity becomes detached from bodily sensation. This explores the frequency of dissociative symptoms in people who had come close to death.

## 11.7 Introduction to Study of NDE and Dissociative Symptoms

Dissociation is the separation of thoughts, feelings, or experiences from the normal stream of consciousness and memory. Examples range from the common non-pathological experiences of daydreaming, to psychogenic amnesia and the "multiple personalities" seen in dissociative identity disorder. Although Janet, who coined the term 'dissociation', viewed it as a discontinuity in awareness caused by stress but rarely experienced by healthy persons, his contemporaries argued that dissociation is a continuous variable present to some degree in everyone. Most modern writers regard dissociation as an adaptive response to intolerable physical or emotional trauma common in otherwise normal people and not necessarily causing high levels of distress. The relation between this common traumatic dissociation and the pathological traits seen in dissociative disorders is controversial. The 4th edition of the American Psychiatric Association's Diagnostic and Statistical Manual of Mental Disorders cautioned that "Dissociation should not be considered inherently pathological and often does not lead to significant distress, impairment, or help-seeking behavior".

Dissociative symptoms have been described in disparate groups of trauma victims, including prisoners, hostages, and rape victims. Some researchers concluded that 25–50% of trauma survivors experience a sense of detachment. In extreme cases, this dissociated perception may lead to amnesia for the trauma or a distorted memory of it.

The dissociative experiences scale (DES) is the most widely used screening instrument for dissociation. There is a 28-item visual analogue scale on which respondents are asked to indicate the percentages of time during which they have different types of dissociative experiences (excluding experiences under the influence of alcohol or drugs). Examples range from the common and non-pathological experience of becoming so absorbed in watching television that the person is unaware of what is happening in the room, to the rare and pathological experiences of having no memory for important past events, or feeling that his or her body belongs to someone else. Individuals with diagnosed dissociative disorders typically have these scores of 30 or higher; most other groups have scores that are very low, often near zero.

Researchers can calculate the percentage of individuals who score 30 or higher, using this as a cutoff for dividing a sample into "high dissociators" and "low dissociators". Although the this includes items relevant to both normal and pathological dissociation, an eight-item subset has been developed as a sensitive measure of purely pathological dissociation.

Some people who come close to death, report having had a profound experience in which they believed they left their physical bodies and transcended the boundaries of the ego and the ordinary confines of time and space. These experiences, often called near-death experiences (NDE)s, include cognitive elements such as accelerated thought processes and a "life review", affective elements such as intense feelings of peace and joy, purportedly paranormal elements such as a sensation of being out of the body or visions of future events, and transcendental elements, such as an experienced encounter with deceased relatives or what is interpreted as an unearthly realm. Although the term near-death experience was not coined until 1975, transcendental experiences near death were reported in the medical literature of the 19th century, and the phenomenon had been described as a discrete syndrome in 1892, when someone published a collection of such cases. A review of all the published estimates concluded that NDEs probably happen to between 9% and 18% of people who have been demonstrably near death.

Several hypotheses have been proposed to explain NDEs; these hypotheses encompass both physiological mechanisms and sociopsychological factors, but the cause remains unclear. Nevertheless, there is a consistent pattern of change in beliefs, attitudes, and values after these experiences. The NDE scale is a 16-item, self-scoring, multiple-choice questionnaire which has documented reliability and validity, and which differentiates NDEs from other responses to a close encounter with death. A score of 7 or higher (of a possible 32) defines an experience as an NDE.

Retrospective studies of people who report NDEs have shown that these individuals are psychologically healthy. However, some people who have NDEs report distress or psychosocial impairment that may be related to difficulty in integrating the experience and its sequelae into their lives.

In the first attempt to understand NDEs psychologically, a researcher proposed that people faced with potentially inescapable danger attempt to avoid this unpleasant reality through pleasurable fantasies. This interpretation was elaborated by others, who viewed the NDE as a type of depersonalization. However, NDEs differ from depersonalization on a number of critical points. A researcher argued that what is altered is not the person's sense of identity, but the association of this identity with bodily sensation. Therefore, he suggested that the NDE is not a type of depersonalization but one of dissociation of the self-identity from bodily sensation and emotions.

Many NDEs include features that are suggestive of dissociation; such features include the partial or total disconnection of the individual's perception experiences, cognitive functioning, emotional state, and sense of identity from the mainstream of the individual's conscious awareness. The epitome of disconnection between the self and the body is the sensation of existing outside the physical body and observing it from another spatial location; this so-called "out-of-body experience" is common in NDEs, and is also described by trauma victims in whom it is seen as a defence against overwhelming physical threat.

It was speculated that people who have NDEs may develop a tendency to dissociate in response to very stressful unforeseen events. Another researcher proposed a developmental theory of sensitivity to extraordinary experiences such as NDEs, in which childhood trauma stimulates the development of a dissociative response as a means of psychological defence. Both these researchers noted, however, that people who have NDEs do not develop a general dissociative defence which they used to cope with everyday stressors, nor do they have a dissociative disorder. The mental health of most such individuals suggests that NDEs are in fact unrelated to clinical dissociative disorders, which are characterized by persistent, recurrent, or chronic dissociation. Although individuals who do meet diagnostic criteria for dissociative disorders may benefit from specific treatments for dissociation, the majority do not have dissociative disorders but nevertheless report dissociative symptoms. Do these individuals have sufficient distress or impairment to warrant similar therapeutic interventions? This article examines the frequency and type of dissociation among a sample of people who had NDEs, and among individuals who came close to death but did not have NDEs.

## 11.8   Methodology of Study and Results of Dissociation of Mind and Body

Participants were recruited from among individuals in order to share accounts of their close brushes with death. Prospective participants were told that the study involved the completion of questionnaires on the specific NDE features that they experienced, and on "several kinds of experiences frequently reported by persons following NDEs … so we can determine whether these experiences are more common among people who have NDEs than among other people."

The study sample included 134 individuals who claimed to have come close to death. 96 (72%) claimed to have had NDEs and described experiences that scored 7 or greater on the NDE scale, and 38 (28%) denied having had NDEs and described experiences that scored less than 7. The two groups were not significantly different in gender distribution, but the individuals who had had NDEs tended to be younger than those who had not.

Because dissociation is often related to previous experiences of trauma. and has been linked to "other worldly" altered states similar to those experiences in NDEs, some have suggested that people who have NDEs, might show high levels of dissociation. This sample of individuals who had had NDEs scored significantly higher on the score than individuals who had come close to death without having had NDEs, but substantially lower than patients with dissociative disorders.

## 11.9   Spiritual Models to explain NDE

Unlike the biological models, spiritual models do not seek biological functions as the primary source for the NDE, though some models do incorporate biological processes into their explanations. Though some spiritual models posit an immortal soul, spiritual realities, or alternative dimensions, others refrain from such speculation. However, what these models all have in common is that they consider the NDE a spiritual experience: they view the NDE as an encounter that should ultimately be defined as metaphysical, that is, entailing existence outside the body.

### 11.9.1   Altered States of Consciousness

One spiritual model that focuses on altered states of consciousness has been proposed in 2001. In this model, the researcher explains that NDEs are biologically-based, algorithmic processes that systematically alter states of consciousness. These altered states carry a dying person through several stages of the dying process in order to (i) convince the person of their passing (the OBE and viewing of their physical body); (ii) produce peace and assurance (the light and feelings of peace); and (iii) prevent resistance to death (being of light and presence of loved ones). The researcher holds that the evolutionary process of natural selection facilitates one's rebirth.

Additionally, the life review provides an important opportunity for the persons to learn from their life before dying and being reborn.

This theory is partially based on a pilot study that he published in 1999. In this study, the researcher obtained seven volunteers from a meeting of the International Association of Near-Death Studies who had had an NDE in the past. He led these volunteers in a guided meditation in which he asked them to imagine a presence behind them and to the left while paying close attention to their breathing. All seven experienced NDE phenomenon, such as feelings of peace and seeing spiritual beings, as a result of the meditation, and many claimed that they were the same features experienced during their actual NDE. Since the altered states of consciousness achieved through meditation produced NDE elements, the researcher posits that NDEs constitute altered states of consciousness.

This researcher includes biological processes as a key feature of his theory by employing another theory of sensed presence. According to this theory, humans have two senses of self, one for each temporal lobe of the brain. If the two lobes slip out of phase the "subordinate right hemisphere's sense of self intrudes into the left side's awareness, and is experienced as an external presence". Thus, biological processes account for the sensed presences and the other phenomena of the NDE. In this way, the researcher's algorithmic reincarnation model interprets the NDE as altered states of consciousness but incorporates a biological element to the theory.

### 11.9.2  Alternate Realities

Though some spiritual models, like this, do not contain an insistence on alternate realities, there are several that do. Theories invoking alternate realities maintain that reality is not confined to the material world; there is much more to the universe than what can be objectively seen, heard, smelled, touched, or tasted.

Alternate reality theories are often paired with the belief that consciousness is at least partially non-local and continues to exist after death. There are many varieties of this view that can be categorized under traditional religious paradigms. Others posit religious significance to the NDE, but do not adhere to any traditional religion. These researchers present less organized and more universalistic religious concepts than their traditional counterparts.

In understanding K. Ring's explanation, it is important to note that he is very clear regarding his interpretation of the NDE: for Ring, the NDE represents reality. He views the OBE as an actual separation of mind from body, or of a spiritual body from a physical one. Likewise, he believes that consciousness continues after death in some type of alternate reality. According to Ring, the NDE is exactly what is described by those who have had one – the beginning stages of transition from this reality to the one that awaits after death. Ring writes:

Most of us, most of the time, function in the three-dimensional world of ordinary sensory reality. According to the interpretation, this reality is grounded in a body-based consciousness. When one quits the body – either at death or voluntarily, as some individuals have learned to do – one's consciousness is then free to explore the fourth-dimensional world.

What is this alternate reality or 'fourth-dimensional world'? Ring surmises that it is a holographic realm made up of pure frequencies. In this 'frequency domain,' individuals perceive and decipher these frequencies holographically. Thus, the OBE and tunnel experience represent the transition in which individuals begin perceiving holographically, and the world of light represents the frequency domain itself. Deceased loved ones will appear in an NDE when the dying person encounters their loved ones' holographic signatures already dwelling in the frequency domain. Interestingly, Ring interprets the being of light that one encounters in the world of light, not as God or any higher spiritual being, but as oneself. It appears infinitely loving and accepting, as well as all-knowing, because it is simply a part of oneself, one's higher self or one's true divine nature. Ring concludes that "the act of dying, then, involves a gradual shift of consciousness from the ordinary world of appearances to a holographic reality of pure frequencies".

# CHAPTER 12

# NEAR-DEATH EXPERIENCE AND CHANGES IN THE BRAIN

## 12.1  What Near-Death Experiences (NDEs) reveal about the Brain?

A young Ernest Hemingway, badly injured by an exploding shell on a World War I battlefield, wrote in a letter home that "dying is a very simple thing. I've looked at death, and really I know. If I should have died it would have been very easy for me. Quite the easiest thing I ever did."

Years later Hemingway adapted his own experience—that of the soul leaving the body, taking flight, and then returning—for his famous short story "The Snows of Kilimanjaro," about an African safari gone disastrously wrong. The protagonist, stricken by gangrene, knows he is dying. Suddenly, his pain vanishes, and Compie, a bush pilot, arrives to rescue him. The two take off and fly together through a storm with rain so thick "it seemed like flying through a waterfall" until the plane emerges into the light: before them, "unbelievably white in the sun, was the square top of Kilimanjaro. And then he knew that there was where he was going." The description embraces elements of a classic near-death experience: the darkness, the cessation of pain, the emerging into the light and then a feeling of peacefulness.

## 12.2  Peace Beyond Understanding

Near-death experiences, or NDEs, are triggered during singular life-threatening episodes when the body is injured by blunt trauma, a heart attack, asphyxia, shock, and so on. About one-in-10 patients with cardiac arrest in a hospital setting undergoes such an episode. Thousands of survivors of these harrowing touch-and-go situations tell of leaving their damaged bodies behind and encountering a realm beyond everyday existence, unconstrained by the usual boundaries of space and time. These powerful, mystical experiences can lead to permanent transformation of their lives.

NDEs are not fancy flights of the imagination. They share broad commonalities—becoming pain-free, seeing a bright light at the end of a tunnel and other visual phenomena, detaching from one's body and floating above it, or even flying off into space (out-of-body experiences). They might include meeting loved ones, living or dead, or spiritual beings such as angels; a Proustian recollection or even review of lifetime memories, both good and bad ("my life flashed in front of my eyes"); or a distorted sense of time and space. There are some underlying physiological explanations for these perceptions, such as progressively narrowing tunnel vision. Reduced blood flow to the visual periphery of the retina means vision loss occurs there first.

NDEs can either be positive or negative experiences. The former receive all the press and relate to the feeling of an overwhelming presence, something numinous, divine. A jarring disconnect separates the massive trauma to the body and the peacefulness and feeling of oneness with the universe. Yet not all NDEs are blissful—some can be frightening, marked by intense terror, anguish, loneliness and despair.

It is likely that the publicity around NDEs has built up expectations about what people should feel after such episodes. It seems possible, in fact, that distressing NDEs are significantly underreported because of shame, social stigma and pressure to conform to the prototype of the "blissful" NDE.

Any close brush with death reminds us of the precariousness and fragility of life and can strip away the layers of psychological suppression that shield us from uncomfortable thoughts of existential oblivion. For most, these events fade in intensity with time, and normality eventually reasserts itself (although they may leave post-traumatic stress disorder in their wake). But NDEs are recalled with unusual intensity and lucidity over decades.

A 2017-study by two researchers at the University of Virginia raised the question of whether the paradox of **enhanced cognition** occurring alongside compromised brain function during an NDE could be written off as a flight of imagination. The researchers administered a questionnaire to 122 people who reported NDEs. They asked them to compare memories of their experiences with those of both real and imagined events from about the same time. The results suggest that the NDEs were recalled with greater vividness and detail than either real or imagined situations were. In short, the NDEs were remembered as being "realer than real."

NDEs came to the attention of the general public in the last quarter of the 20th century from the work of physicians and psychologists—in particular Raymond Moody, who coined the term "near-death experience" in his 1975 best seller, *Life after Life*, and Bruce M. Greyson, one of the two researchers on the study mentioned earlier, who also published The *Handbook of Near-Death Experiences* in 2009. Noticing patterns in what people would share about their near-death stories, these researchers turned a phenomenon once derided as confabulation or dismissed as feverish hallucination (deathbed visions of yore) into a field of empirical study.

These intensely-felt experiences are now accepted as real. They are as authentic as any other subjective feeling or perception. All our thoughts, memories, percepts and experiences are an ineluctable consequence of the natural **causal powers of our brain** rather than of any supernatural ones. That premise has served science and its handmaiden, technology, extremely well over the past few centuries. Unless there is extraordinary, compelling, objective evidence to the contrary, there is no reason to abandon this assumption.

The challenge, then, is to explain NDEs within a natural framework. As a longtime student of the mind-body problem, a researcher said about NDEs because they constitute a rare variety of human consciousness and because of the remarkable fact that an event lasting well under an hour in objective time leaves a permanent transformation in its wake, a Pauline conversion on the road to Damascus—no more fear of death, a detachment from material possessions and an orientation toward the greater good. Or, as in the case of Hemingway, an obsession with risk and death.

Similar mystical experiences are commonly reported when ingesting psychoactive substances from a class of hallucinogens linked to the neurotransmitter serotonin, including psilocybin (the active ingredient in magic mushrooms), LSD, DMT (aka the Spirit Molecule), and 5-MeO-DMT (aka the God Molecule), consumed as part of religious, spiritual or recreational practices.

## 12.3   The Undiscovered Country

It must be remembered that NDEs have been with us at all times in all cultures and in all people, young and old, devout and skeptical (think, for instance, of the so-called *'Tibetan Book of the Dead'*, which describes the mind before and after death). To those raised in religious traditions, Christian or otherwise, the most obvious explanation is that they were granted a vision of heaven or hell, of what awaits them in the hereafter. Interestingly, NDEs are no more likely to occur in devout believers than in secular or nonpracticing subjects.

Personal narratives drawn from the historical record furnish intensely vivid accounts of NDEs that can be as instructive as any dry, clinical case report, if not more so. In 1791, for instance, British admiral Sir Francis Beaufort (after whom the Beaufort wind scale is named) almost drowned, an event he recalled in this fashion:

*"A calm feeling of the most perfect tranquility succeeded the most tumultuous sensation. Nor was I in any bodily pain. On the contrary, my sensations were now of rather a pleasurable cast. Though the senses were thus deadened, not so the mind; its activity seemed to be*

*invigorated in a ratio which defies all description; for thought rose after thought with a rapidity of succession that is not only indescribable, but probably inconceivable, by anyone who has been himself in a similar situation. The course of these thoughts I can even now in a great measure retrace: the event that had just taken place. Thus, traveling backwards, every incident of my past life seemed to me to glance across my recollection in retrograde procession; the whole period of my existence seemed to be placed before me in a kind of panoramic view."*

Another instance was recorded in 1900, when Scottish surgeon Sir Alexander Ogston (discoverer of Staphylococcus) succumbed to a bout of typhoid fever. He described what happened this way:

*"I lay, as it seemed, in a constant stupor which excluded the existence of any hopes or fears. Mind and body seemed to be dual, and to some extent separate. I was conscious of the body as an inert tumbled mass near a door; it belonged to me, but it was not I. I was conscious that my mental-self used regularly to leave the body. I was then drawn rapidly back to it, joined it with disgust, and it became I, and was fed, spoken to, and cared for. And though I knew that death was hovering about, having no thought of religion nor dread of the end, and roamed on beneath the murky skies apathetic and contented until something again disturbed the body where it lay, when I was drawn back to it afresh."*

The underlying neurological sequence of events in a near-death experience is difficult to determine with any precision because of the dizzying variety of ways in which the brain can be damaged. Furthermore, *NDEs do not strike when the individual is lying inside a magnetic scanner or has his or her scalp covered by a net of electrodes.*

It is possible, though, to gain some idea of what happens by examining a cardiac arrest, in which the heart stops beating (the patient is "coding," in hospital jargon). The patient has not died, because the heart can be jump-started via cardiopulmonary resuscitation.

Modern death requires irreversible loss of brain function. When the brain is starved of blood flow (ischemia) and oxygen (anoxia), the patient faints in a fraction of a minute and his or her electroencephalogram, or EEG, becomes isoelectric—in other words, flat. This implies that large-scale, spatially distributed electrical activity within the cortex, the outermost layer of the brain, has broken down. Like a town that loses power one neighborhood at a time, local regions of the brain go offline one after another. The mind, whose substrate is whichever neurons remain capable of generating electrical activity, does what it always does: it tells a story shaped by the person's experience, memory and cultural expectations.

Given these power outages, this experience may produce the rather strange and idiosyncratic stories that make up the corpus of NDE reports. To the person undergoing it, the NDE is as real as anything the mind produces during normal waking. When the entire brain has shut down because of complete power loss, the mind is extinguished, along with consciousness. If and when oxygen and blood flow are restored, the brain boots up, and the narrative flow of experience resumes.

Scientists have videotaped, analyzed and dissected the loss and subsequent recovery of consciousness in highly trained individuals—U.S.-test pilots and NASA astronauts in centrifuges during the cold war. At around five times the force of gravity, the cardiovascular system stops delivering blood to the brain, and the pilot faints. About 10 to 20 seconds after these large g-forces cease, consciousness returns, accompanied by a comparable interval of confusion and disorientation (subjects in these tests are obviously very fit and pride themselves on their self-control).

The range of phenomena these men recount may amount to "NDE-lite"—tunnel vision and bright lights; a feeling of awakening from sleep, including partial or complete paralysis; a sense of peaceful floating; out-of-body experiences; sensations of pleasure and even euphoria; and short but intense dreams, often involving conversations with family members, that remain vivid to them many years afterward. These intensely-felt experiences, triggered by a specific physical insult, typically do not have any religious character (perhaps because participants knew ahead of time that they would be stressed until they fainted).

By their very nature, NDEs are not readily amenable to well-controlled laboratory experimentation, although this might change. For instance, it may be possible to study aspects of them in the humble lab mouse—maybe it, too, can experience a review of lifetime memories or euphoria before death.

## 12.4  Fading of the Light

Many neurologists have noted similarities between NDEs and the effects of a class of epileptic events known as complex partial seizures. These fits partially impair consciousness and often are localized to specific brain regions in one hemisphere. They can be preceded by an aura, which is a specific experience unique to an individual patient that is predictive of an incipient attack. The seizure may be accompanied by changes in the perceived sizes of objects; unusual tastes, smells or bodily feelings; déjà vu; depersonalization; or ecstatic feelings. Episodes featuring on this list are also clinically known as Dostoyevsky's seizures, after the late 19th-century Russian writer Fyodor Dostoyevsky, who suffered from severe temporal lobe epilepsy. Prince Myshkin, the protagonist of his novel The Idiot, remembers:

*"During his epileptic fits, or rather immediately preceding them, he had always experienced a moment or two when his whole heart, and mind, and body seemed to wake up to vigor and light; when he became filled with joy and hope, and all his anxieties seemed to be swept away forever; these moments were but presentiments, as it were, of the one final second (it was never more than a second) in which the fit came upon him. That second, of course, was inexpressible. When his attack was over, and the prince reflected on his symptoms, he used to say to himself: … "What matter though it be only disease, an abnormal tension of the brain, if when I recall and analyze the moment, it seems*

*to have been one of harmony and beauty in the highest degree—an instant of deepest sensation, overflowing with unbounded joy and rapture, ecstatic devotion, and completest life? … I would give my whole life for this one instant."*

More than 150 years later, neurosurgeons are able to induce such ecstatic feelings by electrically stimulating part of the cortex called the insula in epileptic patients who have electrodes implanted in their brain. This procedure can help locate the origin of the seizures for possible surgical removal. Patients report bliss, enhanced well-being, and heightened self-awareness or perception of the external world. Exciting the gray matter elsewhere can trigger out-of-body experiences or visual hallucinations. This brute link between abnormal activity patterns—whether induced by the spontaneous disease process or controlled by a surgeon's electrode—and subjective experience provides support for a biological, not spiritual, origin. The same is likely to be true for NDEs.

Why the mind should experience the struggle to sustain its operations in the face of loss of blood flow and oxygen as positive and blissful rather than as panic-inducing remains mysterious. It is intriguing, though, that the outer limit of the spectrum of human experience encompasses other occasions in which reduced oxygen causes pleasurable feelings of jauntiness, light-headedness and heightened arousal—deepwater diving, high-altitude climbing, flying, the choking or fainting game, and sexual asphyxiation.

Perhaps such ecstatic experiences are common to many forms of death as long as the mind remains lucid and is not dulled by opiates or other drugs given to alleviate pain. The mind, chained to a dying body, visits its own private version of heaven or hell before entering Hamlet's "undiscovered country from whose bourn no traveler returns."

## 12.5   Brain waves of People who had NDE after Cardiac Arrest

Scientists have witnessed brain patterns in dying patients that may correlate to commonly reported near-death" experiences (NDEs) such as lucid visions, out-of-body sensations, a review of one's own life, and other "dimensions of reality. The results offer the first comprehensive evidence that patient recollections and brain waves point to universal elements of NDEs.

During an expansive multi-year study, researchers observed 567 patients in 25 hospitals around the world as they underwent cardiopulmonary resuscitation (CPR) after suffering cardiac arrest, most of which were fatal. Electroencephalogram (EEG) brain signals captured from dozens of the patients revealed that episodes of heightened consciousness occurred up to an hour after cardiac arrest. Though most of the patients in the study were sadly not resuscitated by CPR, 53 patients were brought back to life. Of the survivors, 11 patients reported a sense of awareness during CPR and six reported a near-death experience.

The researchers suggest that the transition from life to death can trigger a state of disinhibition in the brain that "appears to facilitate lucid understanding of new dimensions of reality—including people's deeper consciousness—all memories, thoughts, intentions and actions towards others from a moral and ethical perspective," a finding with profound implications for CPR research, end-of-life care, and consciousness, among other fields.

Patients who survived cardiac arrest "have consistently reported that even though from the perspective of doctors—who try to revive them when they appear to be in a coma and totally unresponsive, teetering between life and death—from their own inner perspective, they find that they're fully conscious. They have an inner experience and their consciousness is not only there but it's heightened to a level that they've never experienced before. Their thoughts become sharper than usual, and clearer than usual."

"Importantly, this experience also involves a purposeful, meaningful reevaluation of their entire life," he continued. "Not just random moments, but the entirety of their life. It's been a mystery, and it's not one or two anecdotes. There have been a number of studies that have suggested maybe up to 10 percent of the adult population is living with one of these experiences, which if you do the mathematics, probably works out to 400 or 500 million people in the world."

Given the sheer ubiquity and common themes of these NDEs, the researchers set out to search for specific **brain waves** in dying people that might be linked to the experiences that are so often reported by survivors of close calls with death. Between 2017 and 2020, the team studied hundreds of comatose patients who were undergoing CPR at hospitals in the United Kingdom and the United States. Getting EEG readings in such an intense environment is understandably challenging, and researchers had to record brain activity in the brief breaks between chest compressions. But they succeeded in capturing transient biomarkers of lucid consciousness in several patients long after initial cardiac arrest.

One of the things that was unique about this project was that this was the first time ever where scientists had put together a method to examine for signs of lucidity and consciousness in people as they're being revived by looking for brain markers, or brain signatures of consciousness, using an EEG device as well as a brain oxygen monitor.

"Most doctors are taught and believe that the brain dies after about five or 10 minutes of oxygen deprivation", the researcher said. "One of the key points that comes out of this study is that that is actually not true. Although the brain flatlines after the heart stops, and that happens within seconds, it doesn't mean that it's permanently damaged and has died. It's just hibernating. What has been shown is that actually, the brain can respond and restore function again, even after an hour later, which opens up a whole window of opportunity for doctors to start new treatments."

Indeed, the study reports that "near-normal/physiological EEG activity (delta, theta, alpha, beta rhythms) consistent with consciousness and a possible resumption of a network-level of cognitive and neuronal activity emerged up to 35-60 minutes into CPR. This is the first report of biomarkers of consciousness during CA/CPR."

These findings are in line with a wave of recent studies focused on the experiences of dying people, which includes reports of surges of brain activity during death, evidence of a gradual shift to death (as opposed to a sudden event), and common themes in near-death experiences.

The researchers also interviewed 28 survivors of cardiac arrest about their brushes with death. The team noted that the vivid experiences that patients report on the border of life and death are highly distinct from dreams and hallucinations that might occur during the days or weeks of recovery from their cardiac arrest.

Indeed, people from all different backgrounds and cultures tend to report near-death experiences with similar elements, such as an out-of-body journey to a comforting place like a childhood home, where the person's life is reviewed in detail through a moral lens, followed by an intuition to return back to the body. The team suggested that these common experiences, which also include glimpses of new dimensions of reality, are triggered by the brain's disinhibition during death, which enables episodes of heightened consciousness that are inaccessible to the living.

"When you looked at the recalled experience of death, and these were actually among a global population, the themes were all consistent", said the researchers. "Our conclusion is that this is a real experience that emerges only with death. As we transition from life to death, somehow, this experience occurs."

## 12.6   Potent Psychedelic DMT can mimic NDE in the Brain

A powerful psychedelic compound found in ayahuasca can model near-death experiences in the brain, a study has found.

Near-death experiences, or NDEs, are significant psychological events that occur close to actual or perceived impending death. Commonly reported aspects of NDEs include out of body experiences, feelings of transitioning to another world and of inner peace, many of which are also reported by users taking DMT (N, N-dimethyltryptamine).

DMT is a potent psychedelic found in certain plants and animals, and is the major psychoactive compound in ayahuasca, the psychedelic brew prepared from vines and leaves and used in ceremonies in south and central America. DMT is a remarkable tool that can enable us to study and thus better understand the psychology and biology of dying.

Researchers from Imperial College London set out to look at the similarities between the DMT experience and reports of NDEs. Their findings, published in the journal *'Frontiers in Psychology'*, reveal a large overlap between those who have had NDEs and healthy volunteers administered DMT.

As part of the trial, the team looked at 13 healthy volunteers over two sessions, who were given intravenous DMT and placebo, receiving one of four doses of the compound. The research was carried out at the NIHR Imperial Clinical Research Facility. All volunteers were screened and overseen by medical staff throughout. Researchers compared the participants' experiences against a sample of people who had previously reported actual NDEs and who had completed a standardized questionnaire to try and quantify their experiences. The group were asked a total of 16 questions including 'Did scenes from your past come back to you?' and 'Did you see, or feel surrounded by, a brilliant light?'.

### 12.6.1   Potent Psychedelic

Following each dosing session, the 13 healthy volunteers filled out exactly the same questionnaire to find out what sort of experiences they had whilst on DMT and how this compared to the NDE group.

The team found that all volunteers scored above a given threshold for determining an NDE, showing that DMT could indeed mimic actual near death experiences and to a comparable intensity as those who have actually had an NDE.

The researchers note some subtle, but important differences between DMT and NDE responses, however. DMT was more likely to be associated with feelings of 'entering an unearthly realm', whereas actual NDEs brought stronger feelings of 'coming to a point of no return'. The team explain that this may be down to context, with volunteers being screened, undergoing psychological preparation beforehand and being monitored through in a 'safe' environment.

"Emotions and context are particularly important in near-death experiences and with psychedelic substances," explains Timmermann. "While there may be some overlap between NDE and DMT-induced experiences, the contexts in which they occur are very different."

## 12.7   Voluntary OBE: an fMRI (Functional Magnetic Resonance Imaging) Study

The present single-case study examined functional brain imaging patterns in a participant who reported being able, at will, to produce somatosensory sensations that are experienced as her body moving outside the boundaries of her physical body all the while remaining aware of her unmoving physical body. It was found that the brain functional changes associated with the reported extra-corporeal experience (ECE) were different than those observed in motor imagery. Activations were mainly left-sided and involved the left supplementary motor area and supramarginal and posterior superior temporal gyri, the last two overlapping with the temporal parietal junction that has been associated with **out-of-body** experiences. The cerebellum also showed activation that is consistent with the participant's report of the impression of movement during the ECE. There was also left middle and superior orbital frontal gyri activity, regions often associated with action monitoring. The results suggest that the ECE reported here represents an unusual type of kinesthetic imagery.

The experience of one's body is a central process to allow us to interact with the outside world. Body experience is based on the integration of visual, vestibular, and somatosensory information. This information allows the tracking of the body in space and in relation with other objects and beings in our environment. Tracking of our body in turn, guides our movements. The conscious experience of our body is generally congruent across sensory modalities so that, what we see of our body is also what we feel from somatosensory and vestibular sensations. The sensations and percept associated with our body in movement can also be elicited in our imagination albeit most of the time in an attenuated form. Motor imagery corresponds to the cognitive version of motor actions without actual motor movements. This motor "imagery" encompass visual components when we imagine movements as we would see them from our own perspective or from a third-person perspective (imagine someone else moving – or imagine ourselves moving but from a third-person perspective) and proprioceptive and vestibular components often referred to kinesthetic "imagery". Motor imagery is intertwined within the brain's preparatory processes preceding action and, up to a certain point, the brain's processes subserving actual movement. The strongest support for this view has come from functional imaging that demonstrated strong but incomplete overlap between imagery, action preparation, and action. These studies show that motor imagery is dependent both on brain regions associated with the performance of motor action but also on the somatosensory brain regions associated with body perception. Voluntary and involuntary motor imagery is also present in amputated individuals with an associated phantom limb often together with somatosensory perception. Some amputees can also train themselves to experience an anatomically impossible movement with their phantom limb suggesting the plasticity of sensorimotor systems.

The multi-component nature of body representation is also revealed in perceptual illusions such as the rubber hand illusion. In the rubber hand illusion, the vision-based belief that the rubber hand is not part of the participant's body is countered by the simultaneous touching of the rubber hand and the real hand and leads to a shift in the attribution of the localization of sensory stimulation from the real hand to the rubber hand. During the process of establishing the illusion, from completely separate to unity with the rubber hand, several intermediate illusory experiences can take place. In one experiment using a moveable hand model, conditions could be manipulated so that participants reported a dissociation of the sense of ownership (impression that the fake hand is their own) or the sense of agency (impression that participants controlled the movements of the fake hand). Mismatch between the observed position of the hand model and the sensed position of the real hand reduced sense of ownership but did not disrupt the impression of agency. Conversely, passive movement reduced agency but left the ownership intact. These observations suggest that agency and ownership may depend on different but overlapping brain networks. Another experiment demonstrated that concurrent limb and full-body orientation illusions elicited by virtual reality visual displacement were undissociated and not dependent on action.

During these illusions, the participants do not doubt that the shifted body perception is illusory. In contrast, shifted body perception of neurological origin or pharmacologically induced can lead to ambiguous embodiment whereas people report that the illusory body or body part is more realistic or corresponds to a "double" of their body.

In the descriptions below, the "double" refers to the illusory body (or parts thereof). There seems to be a general consensus in adopting the classification proposed by a researcher to describe these illusions.

Autoscopic hallucination is a visual hallucination of the upper part of a double of the body. Heautoscopy is a visual and somesthetic hallucination. The double, which appears as through a veil, can mirror the person's movements. Heautoscopy hallucination is also accompanied by a vague feeling of detachment and depersonalization. The double is felt vaguely as another self. Feeling of a presence is a mostly somesthetic hallucination that a double is present usually close by or even touching but not seen. Feeling of a presence is also called sensed-presence experience when the presence is identified as another person. Out-of-body experience is a visual and somesthetic experience in which the double is seen from a different perspective, often motionless. Because the body in this experience is "seen" from a third-person perspective (i.e., from above), the body seen is illusory even if it is congruent with the body's position during the illusion (e.g., lying down). The experience is accompanied by a profound feeling of being outside of the body and with feelings of meaningfulness of the experience.

Three studies of self-reported anomalous body experiences in unremarkable normal people. In the first one, it was noted that most instances of spontaneous anomalous body experiences occurred during a relaxed or borderline sleeping state and one-third reported (seeing) their body from a different perspective while the rest reported a visual or somatosensory shift in perspective. The participants who reported out-of-body experience also self-reported more perceptual anomalies. In two subsequent experiments, participants self-reporting anomalous body experiences (mostly of visual nature) were more likely to respond strongly to aversive visual patterns suggesting that the visual system of the participants are somehow different, at least functionally. These anomalous body experiences depended on temporal lobe anomalies as measured by perceptual tasks and questionnaires.

There also have been imaging enquiries into the brain areas involved in body representation illusions in neurologically intact participants. Brain imaging studies have suggested that activity in sensory integration areas such as the intraparietal sulcus and the ventral premotor cortex are associated with the establishment of the rubber hand illusion. One experiment has used repeated transcranial magnetic stimulation to gain information on the brain areas involved in the rubber hand illusion. It was found that, when the activity of the temporal parietal junction (TPJ) was perturbed by repeated transcranial magnetic stimulation, the processing of body representation mental imagery was impaired. However, in another transcranial magnetic stimulation study, mental rotation of letter stimuli was not affected suggesting a specific effect for body representation. Another experiment showed that, the temporal parietal junction, which is involved in self-processing and multisensory integration of body-related information; and the extra striate body area (EBA), which responds selectively to human bodies and body parts mental imagery is performed with mentally embodied (EBA) or disembodied (TPJ) self-location. The more intense hallucinations or illusions are usually associated with brain lesions, abnormal brain function such as epilepsy, major psychiatric syndromes, dissociative drugs such as ketamine, or in micro-gravity conditions.

The study of the lesioned or abnormal brain areas is often used to gain insight into the brain areas involved in normal body representation phenomena. However, there is also anecdotal evidence that these intense hallucinations can occur in non-neurological cases but they have a low occurrence and, apart from micro-gravity illusions, are unpredictable. In this article, functional MRI was used to examine an otherwise "normal," healthy individual that reported the ability to, at will, vividly experience her body moving outside her physical body while lying down at rest. The subjective description of the participant led to use the term extra-corporeal experience (ECE) throughout this manuscript to underline the difference between the phenomenon studied here and the more common definition of out-of-body experiences. It was included a number of guided imagery tasks to specify the ECE-related brain activity. One control task was motor imagery for a different movement (jumping jacks). A second control condition was alternating between actual finger movements and motor imagery of the same movement.

## 12.8   NDEs and the Mind-Brain Production Theory

Although many 20th-century physicists, psychologists and neuroscientists accepted the reductionistic model that brain produces mind, or indeed is the mind, several features of NDEs call into question whether materialist reductionism will ever provide a full explanation of mind, including and most notably enhanced mental processes, accurate out-of-body perception, and visions of deceased relatives and close friends.

Perhaps the most important of these features, because it is so commonly reported in NDEs, is the occurrence of enhanced mental activity at times when, according to the mind-brain production model, such activity should be diminishing, if not impossible. Individuals reporting NDEs often describe their mental processes during the NDE as remarkably clear and lucid and their sensory experiences as unusually vivid, surpassing those of their normal waking state.

A recent analysis of several hundred NDE cases showed that 80% of experiencers described their thinking during the NDE as "clearer than usual" or "as clear as usual". An analysis of the medical records of people reporting NDEs showed that, in fact, people reported enhanced mental functioning significantly more often when they were actually physiologically close to death than when they were not.

An example of enhanced mental functioning during an NDE is a rapid revival of memories that sometimes extends over the person's entire life. An analysis of several hundred NDEs showed that in 24% of them there was a revival of memories during the NDE. Moreover, in contrast to the isolated and often just single brief memories evoked during cortical stimulation, memories revived during an NDE are frequently described as an almost instantaneous "panoramic" review of the person's entire life.

Another important feature of NDEs that the **mind-brain production theory** cannot adequately account for is the experience of being out of the body (OBE) and perceiving events that one could not ordinarily have perceived. A recent analysis of several hundred cases showed that 48% of NDErs reported seeing their physical bodies from a different visual perspective. Many of them also reported witnessing events going on in the vicinity of their body, such as the attempts of medical personnel to resuscitate them. The mind-brain production theory could attribute the belief that one has witnessed events going on around one's body to a retrospective imaginative reconstruction based on a persisting ability to hear, even when unconscious, or to the memory of objects or events that one might have glimpsed just before losing consciousness or while regaining consciousness, or to expectations about what was likely to have occurred.

Such explanations are inadequate, however, for several reasons. First, memory of events occurring just before or after loss of consciousness is usually confused or completely absent. Second, anecdotal reports that adequately anesthetized patients retain a significant capacity to be aware of or respond to their environment in more than rudimentary ways—let alone to hear and understand— have not been substantiated by controlled studies.

The phenomenology of awakenings under anesthesia is altogether different from that of NDEs, and often extremely unpleasant, frightening, and even painful, typically brief and fragmentary, and primarily auditory or tactile, but not visual. There is no convincing evidence that memories of complex sensory experiences occurring during general anesthesia could have been acquired by the impaired brain itself during the period of unconsciousness.

Furthermore, any such explanatory claims are even less credible when, as commonly happens, the specific sensory channels involved in the reported experience have been blocked as part of the surgical routine—for example, when visual experiences are reported by patients whose eyes were taped shut during the relevant period of time.

A study was carried (in 1982) specifically to examine whether claims of out-of-body perceptions could be attributed to retrospective reconstruction. Patients were interviewed who reported NDEs in which they seemed to be watching what was going on around their body, most of them were cardiac patients who were undergoing cardiopulmonary resuscitation (CPR) at the time of their NDE. "Seasoned cardiac patients" who had not had an NDE during their cardiac-related crises, described a cardiac resuscitation procedure as if they were watching from a third-person perspective. About 80% of the comparison patients made at least one major error in their descriptions, whereas none of the NDE patients made any. Patients who reported leaving their bodies during cardiac arrests described their resuscitations accurately, whereas every cardiac arrest survivor who had not reported leaving the body described incorrect equipment and procedures when asked to describe their resuscitation.

An even more difficult challenge to the mind-brain production theory comes from NDEs in which experiencers report that, while out of the body, they became aware of events occurring at a distance or that in some other way would have been beyond the reach of their ordinary senses even if they had been fully and normally conscious.

In a recent review of 93 published reports of potentially verifiable out-of-body perceptions during NDEs, it was found that 43% had been corroborated to the investigator by an independent informant, an additional 43% had been reported by the experiencer to have been corroborated by an independent informant who was no longer available to be interviewed by the investigator, and only 14% relied solely on the experiencer's report. Of these out-of-body perceptions, 92% were completely accurate, 6% contained some error, and only 1% was completely erroneous. Even among those cases corroborated to the investigator by an independent informant, 88% were completely accurate, 10% contained some error, and 3% were completely erroneous. The cumulative weight of these cases is inconsistent with the conception that purported out-of-body perceptions are nothing more than hallucinations.

There is one particular kind of vision of the deceased that calls into question even more directly their dismissal as subjective hallucinations: cases in which the dying person apparently sees, and often expresses surprise at seeing, a person whom he or she thought was living, who had in fact recently died. Reports of such cases were published in the 19th century and have continued to be reported in recent years. In one recent case, a 9-year-old boy with meningitis, upon awakening from a 36-hour coma, told his parents he had been with his deceased grandfather, aunt, and uncle, and also with his 19-year-old sister who was, as far as his family knew, alive and well at college 500 miles away. Later that day, his parents received news from the college that their daughter had died in an automobile accident early that morning. Because in these cases the experiencers had no knowledge of the death of recently deceased person, the vision cannot plausibly be attributed to the experiencer's expectations.

# CHAPTER 13

# NEAR-DEATH EXPERIENCES AND QUANTUM SCIENCE

## 13.1 Understanding Memories of a Near-death Experience from the Perspective of Quantum Entanglement

Be it the soul in philosophy and religion; the psyche in psychology or the mind or consciousness in science, there seems to be a resilient correlation or similarity with each of these concepts, especially in relation to its preposterousness and absurdity. From a scientific reductionist-based perspective, if we reduce these notions to pure energy generated at the level of subatomic particles that exists all around us, it may seem unswerving (steady of constant). The problematical part is to prove the ability of these entangled subatomic particles to create and store reminiscences outside the body. Quantum studies are now revealing aspects in relations to subatomic particle energy and its ability to perform beyond the imagination of what one can except and visualize. Quantum entanglement is a unique property in quantum physics that best describes the mysterious behaviors that take place at a quantum level with its effects observed at a macroscopic level.

Near-death experiences may be termed absurd by some and hallucinatory by many but there sure is some depth of existence if we look at it from the perspective of quantum generated energy; a pure subatomic energy that exists in the unruly microscopic quantum world; an energy that supports the existence of what we have been addressing as the soul, psyche, mind and consciousness; the oldest form of energy created and present all through the cosmos. With consciousness alone, multiple disciplines have attempted to pinpoint what consciousness is precisely and the best academia has to offer at this point in time is the hard and easy problems of consciousness. Perhaps our lack of understanding of consciousness has inadvertently ruled out the possibility that consciousness does, in fact exist in part outside the brain-body. If it does exist etherically ('ethereal' comes from the Greek word for ether, which means "air" or more specifically "the upper regions of space.") as a field of energy; this may be a game-changer in terms of how we view this phenomenon of the near death-experience (NDE). This article evaluates an experience different from the mainstream and more typical accounts of the near-death experience in that this one was a positive void–based near-death experience and attempts to hypothesize this experience to be a result of quantum entanglement with the interference of the supernatural force that exists beyond the dimensions of space and time.

Before we proceed to explain NDE with the help of 'Quantum Entanglement', Here below is its brief introduction.

## 13.2    A Brief Introduction to Quantum Entanglement

Quantum entanglement is a physical phenomenon that occurs when pairs or groups of particles are generated such that the quantum state of each particle cannot be described independently of the state of the others, even when the particles are separated by a large distance. Measurements of physical properties such as position, momentum, spin, and polarization, performed on entangled particles are found to be correlated.

An entangled system is defined to be one whose quantum state cannot be factored as a product of states of its local constituents; that is to say, they are not individual particles but are an inseparable whole. The state of a composite system is always expressible as a sum, or superposition, of products of states of local constituents; it is entangled if this sum cannot be written as a single product term.

Measurements of physical properties such as position, momentum, spin, and polarization can be performed on the entangled particles. For example, if a pair of entangled particles is generated such that their total spin is known to be zero, and one particle is found to have clockwise spin, then the spin of the other particle will be found to be counterclockwise, thus making the sum of the two spins as 'zero'.

Such phenomena were the subject of a 1935 paper by Albert Einstein, Boris Podolsky, and Nathan Rosen, and several papers by Erwin Schrödinger shortly thereafter, describing what came to be known as the EPR (Einstein-Podolsky-Rosen) paradox. Einstein and others considered such behavior to be impossible, as it violated the local realism view of causality (Einstein referring to it as "spooky action at a distance"). EPR asserted that if such an instant entanglement phenomenon is accepted between the two particles separated by a very large distance; this will violate the maximum limit of the speed of light. Therefore, they argued that the accepted formulation of quantum mechanics must therefore be incomplete. The major nail in the coffin of the EPR paradox came from the physicist John Stewart Bell, in what is known as Bell's Theorem or Bell's inequalities. In experiment-after-experiment, the Bell's inequalities were violated, meaning that quantum entanglement does seem to take place. The final nail in the coffin of the EPR came from some experiments in 1982 by Aspect and his colleagues and the existence of the phenomenon of 'Quantum Entanglement' was conclusively established and the nonlocal nature of quantum entanglement was conclusively established.

## 13.3   What is Nonlocality in Quantum Entanglement?

A non-local connection links up one location with another without crossing space, without decay, and without delay. These connections have three identifying characteristics:

(i)   They are unmediated (no connecting signal is involved, that means it is a signal-less communication);

> (ii)  unmitigated (the strength of the correlations does not fade with increasing distance); and
>
> (iii)  immediate (they are instantaneous).

Basically, the general "principle of locality" requires that "for an action at one point to have an influence at another point, something in the space between the points, such as a field, must mediate the action". In view of the theory of relativity, the speed at which such an action, interaction, or influence can be transmitted between distant points in space cannot exceed the speed of light. This formulation is also known as "Einstein's locality" or "local relativistic causality". It is often stated as "nothing can propagate faster than light, be it energy or merely information" or simply there is "no spooky action-at-a-distance", as Einstein himself put it.

The phenomenon of entanglement between quantum systems raised the nonlocality problem first noted in the EPR paper: A projective measurement on a quantum system at one space location instantly collapses the state of an entangled counterpart at a distant location. Quantum mechanical nonlocality refers to this apparent entanglement-mediated violation of Einstein locality. Although entanglement correlations are affected instantaneously, they cannot be harnessed for faster-than-light communications. The reason is that the outcome of the local projective measurement is itself probabilistic and cannot be predicted beforehand.

Entanglement is a metaphysical-like aspect of quantum mechanics. In simple terms, entanglement maintains that observation of one object can instantaneously influence the behavior of another object, even at very great distances, and even when there appears to be no physical force existing between the two objects. Entanglement is a prime example of the non-local nature of quantum mechanics and is an integral part of the concept of "connectedness" in the universe. In principle, any two objects that have ever interacted are forever entangled– the behavior of one instantaneously influences the other. The meta-physicist would say, "We are all connected in some manner," and in doing so, refer to 'Individual Consciousness' and 'Universal Consciousness', both being integrally one. This is, what is called, Non-duality or Advaita.

Nonlocality is subdivided by some physicists into three types. Type-I is spatial nonlocality; type-II is temporal nonlocality; and type-III nonlocality is both spatial and temporal.

## 13.4 What is 'Spatial Nonlocality' in Quantum Entanglement?

The two (or more) quantumly entangled objects, satisfying the criterion of non-locality, could be located at any distance apart, even galaxies apart. This is called the 'Spatial Nonlocality' in Quantum Entanglement. It is to this type of large separation to which Einstein referred to as 'spooky action' because it violated the phenomenon of the maximum limit of speed of light. Since it is a signal-less transmission, and it is instantaneous, the phenomenon of the maximum limit of speed of light does not apply in this case. So, there is no 'spooky-action-at-a-distance'.

## 13.5 What is 'Temporal Nonlocality' in Quantum Entanglement?

The non-locality of quantum mechanics, as manifested by entanglement, does not apply only to particles with space-like separation, but also to particles with time-like separation. If the two objects are located at two different times (instead of different points in space) and are entangled, this is called 'temporal nonlocality'. It means that the second object (which was generated at a subsequent time) was entangled with the first object which existed in the past, and vice versa. The future, past, present, and consciousness are entangled within the quantum continuum. So, *there is no difference between the past, present, or future in this case.*

## 13.6    Perception of Time and Nonlocality

Time is a concept that spans the human condition. Psychological research shows that just about all of human experience is dependent upon and influenced by how individuals perceive time, localize themselves consciously within space and time and process their temporally-based perceptions and experiences. Classical physics has successfully allowed us to calculate and measure time at the macroscale while relativistic physics demonstrates how time and space are conjugate pairs that manifest in a unified continuum. With the establishment of quantum mechanics, concepts such as entanglement and nonlocality allow us to construct a new cosmological model of time that connects with cognitive perception—one that asserts that time is perceived in a complementary timeful and timeless state. In the timeful state, the mind perceives time in its localized, linear, and causal aspects; while in its timeless state as non-local, symmetrical, and entangled. Many of the spiritual traditions throughout history maintain a similar position of human consciousness as having the capacity to abide within these complementary modes of existence. How time, and conceptions about **the past, present or future are therefore illusions**, as there is no 'future' or 'past'. However, when considered from the perspective of quantum mechanics, time-space is a continuum, a unity, and time does not exist independent of this continuum, except as an act of perceptual registration by consciousness or mechanical means.

The recognition of the mind's ability to experience both the localized and non-localized complementary aspects of time was the impetus for the ancient mystics to develop advanced mental techniques to master time within the domain of human consciousness. The goal of these disciplines was to liberate from the inherent cognitive filters that limit one's consciousness into the distorted and fragmented perception of time.

The mechanism that reduces human consciousness into experiencing time in its temporally localized state is what is referred to as veiled non-locality. The term implies how consciousness disguises its wholeness and nonlocality in order to produce local processes. This filtering process allows for specific observations and thoughts in a classical world of everyday experience, while keeping quantum and general relativistic processes out of sight.

## 13.7   Time is Entangled

Time cannot be separate from the continuum except when perceived as such by an observing consciousness or measuring device, thereby inducing a collapse of the wave function of time; experienced as the present, past, or future. Time, be it considered a dimension known as time-space, or as a perceived aspect of the quantum continuum, is also subject to entanglement, as all aspects of time are interconnected and indistinguishable until perceived thereby inducing a collapse of the wave function. "A" future can therefore effect "a" past and change it through entanglement and by influencing the wave function.

The quantum continuum is without dimensions and encompasses space and time in its basic unity of oneness. Everything within the quantum continuum can be influenced by the local effect and distant effects simultaneously at and beyond light speeds. Therefore, the future, and the "present" being part of this continuum can influence the past by effecting the wave function of the past, present, future, and thus, the space-time continuum, as all are entangled. Time-space is interactional, and can contract to near nothingness and then continue to contract in a negative direction such that the time traveler can journey into the past.

## 13.8   Quantum Secrets of Life After Death

What happens to us when we die? This is one of the most profound and enduring questions that humans have ever asked. Many religions and philosophies have offered their own answers, but none of them can be proven or disproven by science. However, some scientists have suggested that quantum physics, the branch of physics that deals with the smallest and most mysterious aspects of reality, may offer some clues about the nature of consciousness and the possibility of life after death.

Quantum physics is notoriously difficult to understand and explain, but one of its most intriguing features is the phenomenon of **quantum entanglement**. This is when two particles, such as photons or electrons, become so intimately linked that they share the same quantum state, even when they are separated by vast distances. This means that whatever happens to one particle instantly affects the other, regardless of any physical barriers or laws of causality. Albert Einstein famously called this "spooky action at a distance".

Some scientists have speculated that quantum entanglement may play a role in the formation and preservation of consciousness, which is the subjective experience of being aware and alive. They argue that consciousness may not be confined to the brain, but may be a fundamental property of the universe, like energy or matter. According to this view, consciousness may be composed of quantum information that can exist and persist beyond the physical body, and may even transcend space and time.

One of the proponents of this idea is **Dr. Stuart Hameroff**, a professor of anesthesiology and psychology at the University of Arizona. He has collaborated with **Sir Roger Penrose**, a renowned physicist and mathematician, to develop a theory called orchestrated objective reduction (Orch-OR). This theory proposes that **quantum vibrations in microtubules**, which are tiny structures inside brain cells, are responsible for generating and maintaining consciousness. These quantum vibrations may also be entangled with other quantum systems in the universe, forming a kind of quantum network that connects all conscious beings.

According to Hameroff and Penrose, when a person dies, their brain stops functioning and their quantum information dissipates into the environment. However, this does not mean that their consciousness is destroyed. Instead, their quantum information may remain entangled with other quantum systems in the universe, and may even undergo a process of quantum collapse that leads to a new level of consciousness. In other words, death may not be the end, but rather a transition to a different state of existence.

Hameroff points to the single-celled paramecium as evidence. The paramecium has no central nervous system, no brain, no neurons, but it swims, locates food, finds a mate, and avoids danger. It seems to make choices, and it definitely seems to process information. And since microtubules are nanoscale structures, Hameroff also began thinking that quantum physics might play a role in consciousness and the mind.

For some people, the idea that quantum physics may offer a glimpse into the mystery of death is fascinating and comforting. It may provide them with a sense of hope and wonder, and a feeling that there is more to reality than meets the eye. It may also inspire them to explore their own consciousness and its connection to the cosmos, and to seek deeper understanding and wisdom in their lives.

But how can we test this idea? Is there any way to verify or falsify it? Can we ever know for sure what happens after we die? Some researchers have proposed various experiments and methods to investigate the quantum nature of consciousness and its survival after death. For example, some have suggested using near-death experiences (NDEs), which are reported by some people who have been clinically dead or close to death, as possible evidence for quantum consciousness. Others have proposed using quantum computers or artificial intelligence to simulate or emulate consciousness and its interactions with quantum systems.

However, these approaches face many challenges and limitations. For one thing, NDEs are subjective and anecdotal experiences that cannot be easily replicated or controlled in a scientific setting. They are also influenced by cultural and psychological factors that may affect their interpretation and validity. For another thing, quantum computers and artificial intelligence are still in their infancy stages and have not yet reached the level of complexity and sophistication required to model or mimic consciousness. They also raise ethical and philosophical questions about the nature and value of artificial life.

Therefore, it seems that we are still far from finding definitive answers to the question of life after death using quantum physics. However, this does not mean that we should give up on our quest for knowledge and meaning. On the contrary, it means that we should embrace the uncertainty and mystery of our existence and keep an open mind and a curious spirit. Quantum physics may not give us definitive answers, but it may give us new perspectives and possibilities to explore and appreciate. It may also remind us that we are part of a larger and more mysterious reality than we can imagine, and that we are connected to each other and to the universe in profound and subtle ways.

Perhaps, in the end, the question of life after death is not so much about finding a final destination or a definitive answer, but about finding a way to live fully and meaningfully in the present moment, and to appreciate the beauty and wonder of life in all its forms and expressions. Perhaps, as the physicist Richard Feynman once said, "The mystery of life is not a problem to be solved, but a reality to be experienced."

## 13.9    Quantum Effects of Microtubules

Communication at the level of microtubules has been described mathematical. A growing body of scientific knowledge supports the theory that **microtubules** possess three important properties related to intercellular and intracellular communications: (a) propagation of laser-like, coherent micropulses of light; (b) quantum, non-local information processing; and (c) emergent, collective, macroscopic properties arising from a critical level of coherence of quantum events.

### 13.9.1    Light Propagation

Microtubules propagate laser-like, coherent, single-photon micropulses of light that result from Bose-Einstein condensation. Evidence suggests that these individual micropulses of light effectively generate single-photon holograms, just as a laser beam, composed of countless individual photons, generates a hologram. If trillions of microtubules in the human body each create single-photon holograms, the amount of holographically encoded information may be effectively unlimited. However, unlike other Bose Einstein condensates, these occur at body temperature. Their energy source is the 98.6 ambient heat bath of human cellular fluids, or cytoplasm, in which microtubules are immersed. Cells filled with cytoplasm are not simply minuscule bags of water with organelles sloshing around randomly. Rather, cytoplasm is a highly structured viscous fluid that has evolved to allow rapid communication through its unique electromagnetic and quantum properties-through microtubules. The human body is thus possessed of collective quantum effects throughout its entirety, including, most importantly, the central nervous system and the brain. The implication is that vast quantities of information about the state of the organism and its environment can be absorbed and re-emitted by single photons.

### 13.9.2   Non-local Communication

A second inherent property of micro tubules is the quantum phenomenon of non-local communication, or so called "action-at-a-distance." Researchers described microtubule signal propagation within the human body as occurring instantaneously. Non-local communication is implicated in many subjectively reported **altered-state experiences such as near-death life reviews**. Such reports are not in accord with classical concepts of linear time and space. The microtubule network may provide the communication mechanism for instantaneous downloading of an entire lifetime of experiences that are "replayed" in a matter of moments, as if the process occurs at a highly accelerated rate. Note that we are not referring to the familiar neurochemical signal propagation within the central nervous system, which travels at approximately 240 miles per hour. Indeed, we are referring to a related, yet clearly distinct, communications network.

### 13.9.3  Emergent Properties

Finally, consider that emergent, collective, macroscopic properties may arise from a critical level of coherence of quantum events. The laser, a room-temperature Bose-Einstein condensate, is an example. The photons arising from the absorption and re-emission of stimulating energy give rise to the collective coherent effect of an intense beam of light of a single wavelength. In this model, microtubules function as pulse-laser signal generators possessing weak electromagnetic fields that cross over between microtubules. Cross-over between any two microtubules situated parallel to one another would result in interference patterns, similar to bands of dark and light. Encoded within the interference patterns would be enormous quantities of holographic information. It is well known that anesthetics impair the functioning of microtubules, an effect that leads to loss of consciousness. Such evidence indicates that microtubules may represent the physical structures responsible for the emergence of consciousness. The net effect of countless bundles of neuronal microtubule "cables" would thus be the basis for a profound emergent collective, macroscopic effect: consciousness. Emergence refers to the occurrence of conscious awareness at a critical threshold-resulting from the cumulative effect of countless microtubules acting in a coordinated manner. Consciousness is thus said to result from collective quantum effects that occur in microtubule networks within the central nervous system. Moreover, experimental research links microtubules to bioinformation processes such as memory and learning. For example, in Alzheimer's disease, the cytoskeleton-the microtubule network-becomes entangled. The clinical symptoms of Alzheimer's disease, that is, cognitive defects in learning and memory, have been produced and studied by the drug colchicine, which causes selective destruction of brain microtubules. **Near-death life reviews within the context of this model represent a specific, emergent, quantum effect that is both collective and macroscopic.**

# BIBLIOGRAPHY


**Agrillo,** C. (2011). "Near-Death Experience: Out-of-Body and Out-of-Brain?, Review of General Psychology, 15(1), 1–10. https://doi.org/10.1037/a0021992

**Beck,** T.E., Colli, J.E. "A Quantum Biomechanical Basis for Near-Death Life Reviews". Journal of Near-Death Studies 21, 169–189 (2003). https://doi.org/10.1023/A:1021292006371

**Blackmore,** Susan. "Beyond the body. An investigation of out-of-body experiences", Academy Chicago Publishers, 1992.

**Blanke,** Olaf; and Sebastian Dieguez. "Leaving Body and Life Behind: Out-of-Body and Near-Death Experience", The Neurology of Consciousness, 2009, pp. 303-325. Elsevier Ltd.

**Blanke,** Olaf; Theodor Landis; Laurent Spinelli; and Margitta Seeck. " Out-of-body experience and autoscopy of neurological origin", Brain, Volume 127, Issue 2, February 2004, Pages 243–258, https://doi.org/10.1093/brain/awh040.

**Burke,** John. "Imagine Heaven: Near-Death Experiences, God's Promises, And the Exhilarating Future That Awaits You", Baker Academic, 2015.

**Burpo,** Todd; and Lynn Vincent. "Heaven Is for Real: A Little Boy's Astounding Story of His Trip to Heaven and Back", Thomas Nelson Publishers, 2010.

**Bush,** Nancy Evans; and Bruce Greyson. "Distressing Near-Death Experiences: The Basics", Mo Med. 2014 Nov-Dec; 111(6): 486–491. PMCID: PMC6173534PMID: 25665233

**Cicoria,** Tony, and Jordan Cicoria "Getting Comfortable with Near-Death Experiences: My Near-Death Experience A Telephone Call from God", Mo Med. 2014 Jul-Aug; 111(4): 304–307.

PMCID: PMC6179462PMID: 25211856,

**Eadie,** Betty, J. "Embraced by the Light", Simon & Schuster, 1993.

**Facco,** Enrico; and Edoardo Casiglia; Benedikt Emanuel Al Khafaji; Francesco Finatti; Gian Marco Duma; Giovanni Mento; Luciano Pederzoli; and Patrizio Tressoldi. "Neurophenomenology of Out-of-Body Experiences Induced by Hypnotic Suggestions", Hypnosis and Out-of-Body Experiences, Int J Clin Exp Hypn. 2019 Jan-Mar; 67(1): 39-68.

doi: 10.1080/00207144.2019.1553762.

**French,** Christopher C. "Near-death experiences in cardiac arrest survivors", Progress in Brain Research, Volume 150, 2005, Pages 351-367.

**Greyson,** Bruce. "Dissociation in people who have near-death experiences: out of their bodies or out of their minds?", The Lancet, Volume 355, Issue 9202, 2000, Pages 460-463, https://doi.org/10.1016/S0140-6736(00)82013-9.

**Greyson,** Bruce. "Cosmological Implications of Near-Death Experiences", Journal of Cosmology, 2011, Vol. 14, pp. 4684-4696.

**Greyson,** Bruce. "Incidence and correlates of near-death experiences in a cardiac care unit", Gen Hosp Psychiatr. 25: 269 – 276, 2003.

**Greyson,** Bruce and Stevenson, I. "The phenomenology of near-death experiences", Am. J Psychiatr. 137: 1193-1196, 1980.

**Greyson,** Bruce; et. al. "Electromagnetic Phenomena Reported by Near-Death Experiencers", Journal of Near-Death Studies, 33(4), pp. 213-243. Summer 2015.

**Hashemi,** Amirhossein; Ali Akbar Oroojan; Maryam Rassouli, and Hadis Ashrafizadeh. "Explanation of near-death experiences: a systematic analysis of case reports and qualitative research", Front. Psychol., 20 April 2023, Sec. Consciousness Research, Volume 14 – 2023, https://doi.org/10.3389/fpsyg.2023.1048929.

**Irwin,** H.J. "Flight of Mind: A Psychological Study of the Out-of-Body Experience", 1985, Metuchen, NJ: The Scarecrow Press Inc.

**Jayaram,** V. "What happens after death?", Durgadharma, February 11, 2017. http://www.hinduwebsite.com,

**Kelly,** E.W. "Near-death experiences with reports of meeting deceased people", Death Stud, 25: 229-249, 2001.

**Koch,** Christof, "What Near-Death Experiences Reveal about the Brain" Scientific American, June 1, 2020.

**Kohr,** R.L. "Near-death experiences, altered states, and psi sensitivity", J. Near Death Stud, 3:157-176, 1983.

**Lundahl,** Craig R. "Near-Death Studies and Modern Physics", Journal of Near-Death Studies, 18(3) Spring 2000, pp. 143-179.

**Maarive,** "7 minutes of afterlife: A 60-year-old's revelation and return from death", Jerusalem Post, August 31, 2023.

**Menon,** Murli. "Near Death Experience of a Hindu: Moments that change you forever", hackwriters.com, January 07, 2023.

**Menon,** Murli. "ZeNLP- the power to relax: Tribal meditation techniques for stress Management (ZeNLP- learning through stories), Sage Publications.

**Moody,** Raymond, A. "Life After Life: The Investigation of a Phenomenon- Survival of Body Death", Rider (Random House), 2001.

**Moorjani,** Anita. "Dying to be Me: My Journey from Cancer to Near Death, to True Healing", Hay House, 2012.

**Neal,** Mary C. "7 Lessons from Heaven", Convergent Books, 2017.

**Nelson,** Kevin. "The Spiritual Doorway to the Brain: A Neurologist's Search for the God Experience", Dutton, 2010.

**Pandarakalam,** Dr. James Paul. "A Search for the Truth of Near-Death Experiences" https://www.rcpsych.ac.uk/docs/default-source/members/sigs/spirituality-spsig/a-search-for-the-truth-of-ndes-ja

**Pasricha,** Satwant and Ian Stevenson. "Near-Death Experiences in India: A Preliminary Report", The Journal of Nervous and Mental Disease, Vol. 174, No. 3, 1986, pp. 165-170.

**Pattanaik,** Devdutt. "What exactly happens after death according to Hinduism?", Soulveda, 27 July 2019.

**Pereira,** Contzen and Janice Harter. "Understanding memories of a near-death experience from the perspective of quantum entanglement and in the presence of the supernatural", Journal of Metaphysics and Connected Consciousness, 12 January 2016.

**Purkayastha,** Moushumi and Kanchan Kumar Mukherjee. "Three cases of near-death experience: Is it physiology, physics or philosophy?", Ann Neurosci. 2012 Jul; 19(3): 104–106. doi: 10.5214/ans.0972.7531.190303.

**O'Hare,** Ryan. "Potent psychedelic DMT mimics near-death experience in the brain", Imperial College London News 15 Aug 2018.

**Ring,** K. "Life at Death: A Scientific Investigation of the Near-Death Experience", 1980. New York: Conward, McCann & Geoghegan.

**Sabom,** M.B. "Recollections of Death: A Medical Investigation", 1982, New York: Harper & Row.

**Sluijs,** Marinus van der. "Three Ancient Reports of Near-Death Experiences: Bremmer Revisited", Journal of Near-Death Studies, 27(4), Summer 2009, pp. 223-253.

**Smith,** Andra M., Claude Messier Front. Hum. Neurosci., 10 February 2014, Sec. Sensory Neuroscience, Voluntary out-of-body experience: an fMRI study", Volume 8, 2014. https://doi.org/10.3389/fnhum.2014.00070.

**Stockton,** Shona. "Near-Death Experience in Indian Religions: Encountering Yama", M.A. Dissertation, University of Chester, United Kingdom, 2017.

**Shushan,** Gregory. "Near-death experiences have long inspired afterlife beliefs", Continuum (Bloomsbury) Advances in Religious Studies, 2011.

**Van Lommel**, P. et al. "Near-death experience in survivors of cardiac arrest: A prospective study in the Netherlands". Lancet 358: 2039 – 2045, 2001.

**Verney,** Thomas R. "4 Theories That Could Explain Near-Death Experiences", Psychology Today> April 01, 2022.

**Wallace,** Holly. "Near-Death Experiences, Religion, and Life After Death", M.A. Dissertation, University of South Florida, April 8, 2004. https://digitalcommons.usf.edu/etd/1288.